# DINOSAURS

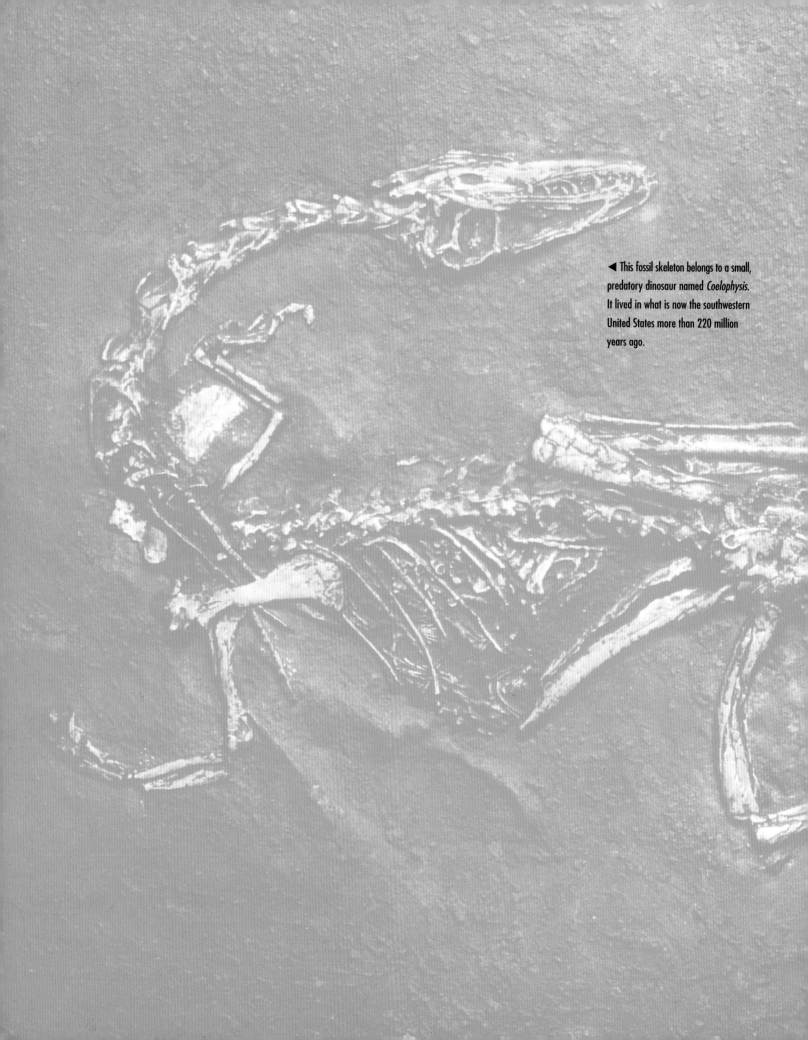

◄ This fossil skeleton belongs to a small, predatory dinosaur named *Coelophysis*. It lived in what is now the southwestern United States more than 220 million years ago.

# DINOSAURS

## Nigel Marven

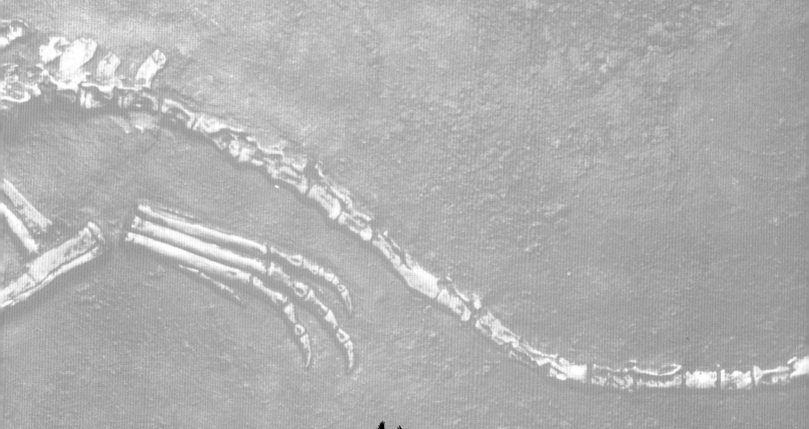

KINGFISHER

BOSTON

Additional text: Dougal Dixon
Editor: Clare Hibbert
Coordinating editors: Caitlin Doyle, Stephanie Pliakas
Designers: Peter Clayman, Rebecca Painter
Consultant: Dr. Phil Manning, School of Earth, Atmospheric and
  Environmental Sciences, University of Manchester, England
Picture research manager: Cee Weston-Baker
Senior production controller: Lindsey Scott
DTP manager: Nicky Studdart
DTP operator: Claire Cessford
Proofreaders: Polly Goodman, Denise Heal
Indexer: Polly Goodman

KINGFISHER
a Houghton Mifflin Company imprint
222 Berkeley Street
Boston, Massachusetts 02116
www.houghtonmifflinbooks.com

First published in 2007
10 9 8 7 6 5 4 3 2 1

1TR/0607/TWP/MA(MA)/130ENSOMA/F

ISBN: 978-0-7534-6102-0

Marven, Nigel.
  Kingfisher knowledge: dinosaurs / Nigel Marven.—1st ed.
    p.  cm.
  Includes index.
  1. Dinosaurs—Juvenile
  literature. I. Title.
  QE861.5.M3429 2007
  567.9—dc22
              2007020006
Printed in Singapore

**GO FURTHER . . .**
INFORMATION PANEL KEY:

web sites and
further reading

career paths

places to visit

# Contents

Foreword                         6


CHAPTER 1
WORLD OF DINOSAURS      7

Dinosaur families              8–9
Changing continents          10–11
Why dinosaurs died out    12–13
Summary                          14

**NOTE TO READERS**
The web site addresses listed in this book are correct at the time of going to print. However, due to the ever-changing nature of the Internet, web site addresses and content can change. Web sites can contain links that are unsuitable for children. The publisher cannot be held responsible for changes in web site addresses or content, or for information obtained through third-party web sites. We strongly advise that Internet searches are supervised by an adult.

▼ Plesiosaurs were large marine reptiles that swam in the world's waters from around 200 million years ago until 65 million years ago.

## CHAPTER 2
## EURASIA 15

The first dinosaur hunters 16–17
The fossil record 18–19
Fighting dinosaurs 20–21
Feathered dinosaurs 22–23
Flying reptiles 24–25
Marine reptiles 26–27
Summary 28

## CHAPTER 3
## THE AMERICAS 29

Hunting in packs 30–31
Armored dinosaurs 32–33
Famous giants 34–35
Hell Creek today 36–37
Hell Creek long ago 38–39
Hadrosaurs 40–41
Titanosaur nursery 42–43
Warm- or cold-blooded? 44–45
Summary 46

## CHAPTER 4
## AFRICA & AUSTRALIA 47

Dinosaur teeth 48–49
Fast-moving plant eaters 50–51
Madagascan giant 52–53
Dinosaur tracks 54–55
Polar dinosaurs 56–57
Summary 58

Timeline 59

Glossary 60–61
Index 62–63
Acknowledgments 64

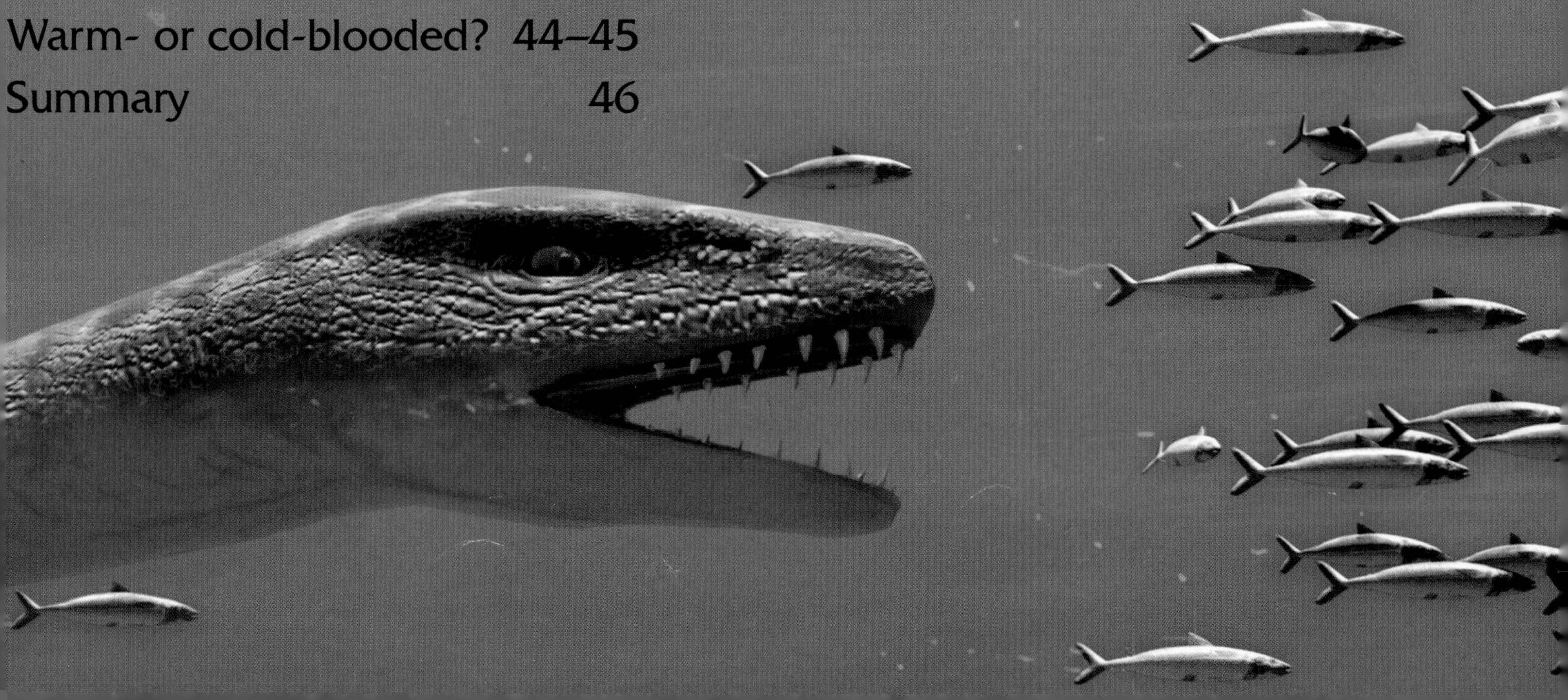

# Foreword

Dinosaur—one of the most thrilling words in the English language! It conjures up images of a prehistoric past when the world was ruled by great reptiles. Some were ferocious predators; others, gentle giants. This book provides a glimpse of their world. I became interested in dinosaurs because of my passion for smaller reptiles. Ever since I can remember, I've had a menagerie of cold-blooded pets, from geckos to giant tortoises. It's wonderful to think that some of today's reptiles were around during dinosaur times. And when I watch my lizards feeding, displaying to each other, or laying eggs, they give clues to how dinosaurs behaved.

My job as a wildlife TV host gave me a chance to get even closer to dinosaurs. The makers of *Walking with Dinosaurs* asked if I could join them to travel back in time to meet computer-generated *Tyrannosaurus rex*, *Protoceratops*, *Argentinosaurus*, plesiosaurs, and more. They needed a person to give scale to their creations, and many of the creatures that I came to know so well are featured in this book. To get our facts right, we relied on teams of paleontologists (dinosaur experts). I learned so much about the Triassic, Jurassic, and Cretaceous—the periods when Earth was dominated by dinosaurs.

Of course, without a time machine, nobody can be sure how dinosaurs looked. As you'll see on page 40, dinosaur scales are occasionally preserved, but fossils never reveal the true colors of their skin, so we can't tell if dinosaurs were green, brown, orange, red, or blue. But by seeing how modern animals camouflage themselves or get dazzling colors in the breeding season, we can make reasonable guesses. Sounds don't fossilize either, so we don't know if *Tyrannosaurus rex* roared or if *Triceratops* bellowed, but fossils do give clues about dinosaur calls, as you'll see on page 41.

Making the television shows also gave me an insight into dinosaur habitats. The filmmakers tried to choose landscapes with just the right vegetation. Grass would never do—it didn't evolve until long after dinosaurs became extinct. Monkey-puzzle trees are perfect because their close relatives have been around for some 300 million years. To film the right background for my adventures with *Tyrannosaurus rex*, we went to Chile in South America, the home of some of the last remaining monkey-puzzle forests.

Fraser Island in Australia is another good substitute for prehistoric landscapes. It has vast sand dunes that look exactly like the Mongolian deserts inhabited by *Protoceratops* and *Velociraptor*. You can read about a famous fossil of these two dinosaurs fighting on page 21. Fraser Island also has forests of cycads and tree ferns, ancient plants that were eaten by dinosaurs. Page 39 describes some other greenery that they ate.

While researching the dinosaur programs, I was stunned by an exciting revelation: dinosaurs aren't actually extinct! You can read the evidence for this on page 23. Most paleontologists now agree that dinosaurs evolved into birds. Their skeletons are so similar that some fossil dinosaurs have been mistaken for birds and vice versa. So when you're immersed in the dinosaur world that this book reveals, don't be too disappointed that they're long gone. Dinosaurs are still here right now, flying from tree to tree in your backyard or local park.

*Nigel Marven*

Nigel Marven, naturalist and filmmaker and wildlife consultant on the BBC's *Walking with Dinosaurs* television special

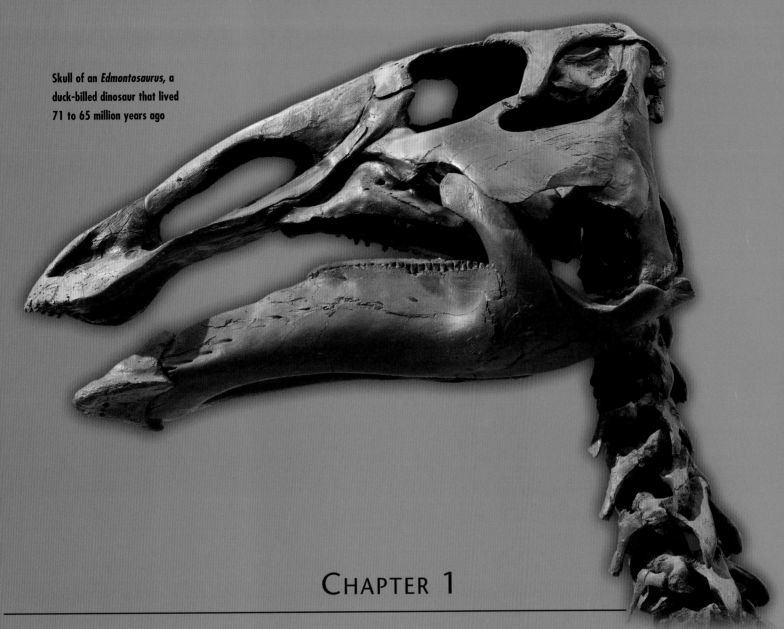

Skull of an *Edmontosaurus*, a duck-billed dinosaur that lived 71 to 65 million years ago

## CHAPTER 1

# World of dinosaurs

When we imagine a dinosaur, we usually picture a big animal—an enormous plant eater with a long neck or a dragonlike meat eater with sharp teeth and a fearsome temper. These images are not wrong, but they do not tell the whole story. Since the discovery of dinosaurs almost 200 years ago, our ideas about these prehistoric reptiles have continued to change. Every year, almost every week, fresh information comes to light. This new evidence includes fossilized remains as well as other clues about how dinosaurs lived and what sort of world they inhabited. Paleontology, the study of ancient life, is a thriving science, and the study of dinosaur fossils is an important part of this. Thanks to the work of paleontologists, we now understand the world of dinosaurs better than ever before.

Argentinosaurus

# Dinosaur families

D escended from a single ancestor, dinosaurs eventually evolved into more than 1,000 different species. Large or small, plant-eating or predatory, dinosaurs had many differences, but they also shared certain characteristics. Many walked on their toes, and they all had limbs that came straight down from their bodies rather than out from their sides, like those of many modern reptiles.

◄ Dinosaurs ranged in size from tiny predators to colossal plant eaters. *Compsognathus*, a speedy hunter, weighed less than 6.6 lbs. (3kg). At the other end of the scale, *Argentinosaurus* was a lumbering plant eater, as tall as a four-story building.

## Great and small

Straight legs can support a heavy body better than bent legs can. Just imagine if an elephant had legs that stuck out at the side like a lizard! Not only would it look silly, but it would not have the strength to lift its bulky body. Even the smallest dinosaurs had straight legs. Chicken-size *Compsognathus* evolved from much bigger dinosaurs and kept the straight legs of its ancestors.

Compsognathus

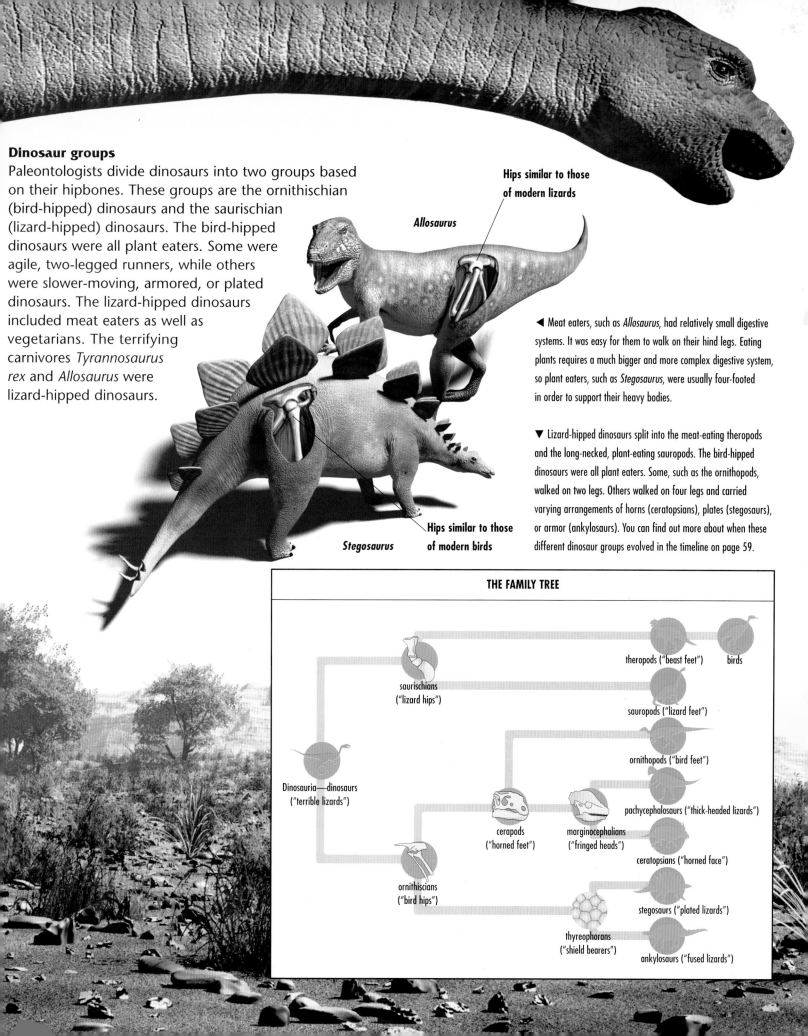

## Dinosaur groups

Paleontologists divide dinosaurs into two groups based on their hipbones. These groups are the ornithischian (bird-hipped) dinosaurs and the saurischian (lizard-hipped) dinosaurs. The bird-hipped dinosaurs were all plant eaters. Some were agile, two-legged runners, while others were slower-moving, armored, or plated dinosaurs. The lizard-hipped dinosaurs included meat eaters as well as vegetarians. The terrifying carnivores *Tyrannosaurus rex* and *Allosaurus* were lizard-hipped dinosaurs.

**Hips similar to those of modern lizards**

*Allosaurus*

◀ Meat eaters, such as *Allosaurus*, had relatively small digestive systems. It was easy for them to walk on their hind legs. Eating plants requires a much bigger and more complex digestive system, so plant eaters, such as *Stegosaurus*, were usually four-footed in order to support their heavy bodies.

▼ Lizard-hipped dinosaurs split into the meat-eating theropods and the long-necked, plant-eating sauropods. The bird-hipped dinosaurs were all plant eaters. Some, such as the ornithopods, walked on two legs. Others walked on four legs and carried varying arrangements of horns (ceratopsians), plates (stegosaurs), or armor (ankylosaurs). You can find out more about when these different dinosaur groups evolved in the timeline on page 59.

*Stegosaurus*

**Hips similar to those of modern birds**

### THE FAMILY TREE

saurischians ("lizard hips")

theropods ("beast feet")     birds

sauropods ("lizard feet")

Dinosauria—dinosaurs ("terrible lizards")

ornithopods ("bird feet")

pachycephalosaurs ("thick-headed lizards")

cerapods ("horned feet")

marginocephalians ("fringed heads")

ceratopsians ("horned face")

ornithiscians ("bird hips")

stegosaurs ("plated lizards")

thyreophorans ("shield bearers")

ankylosaurs ("fused lizards")

# Changing continents

The world of the earliest dinosaurs would have been unrecognizable to later species. When dinosaurs first appeared, there was only one big landmass on Earth. Over time, this split apart into the continents that we know today. Unable to cross oceans, dinosaur populations became cut off, and completely new species evolved. Asia's ceratopsian (or horned) dinosaurs, for example, looked very different from North America's famous *Triceratops*.

### An island continent

During the Cretaceous period (145 to 65 million years ago, or m.y.a.), South America was like Australia is today—a massive continent completely surrounded by water. Also like Australia today, it had its own unique animal life, different from animal life anywhere else. The long-necked sauropods continued to be the main plant eaters in South America after they had largely been replaced elsewhere by the duck-billed dinosaurs.

### World on the move

How could continents move apart and break up? Earth's landmasses sit on large rafts of rock, called plates, that are constantly moving. Over millions of years, continents drift, and oceans widen or close. This means that different time periods have very different physical geography and, as a result, very different climates, too.

230 m.y.a.  160 m.y.a.  65 m.y.a.

▲ These maps show the landmasses and oceans at different times during the history of the dinosaurs. At 230 m.y.a., all of the land was clumped into one big supercontinent called Pangaea. Slowly, at a rate of around 1 in. (2cm) per year, Pangaea broke apart into the continents that we know today. People who study how continents change are called paleogeographers.

▼ *Triceratops* was a ceratopsian dinosaur that evolved in North America during the Cretaceous period. Its name means "three-horned face." *Triceratops* lived alone or in family groups.

▲ The Triassic period lasted from 250 m.y.a. to 208 m.y.a. The single Triassic continent had a hot, dry climate. The interior was so far from the ocean that it was an uninhabitable desert. Life existed only around the edges, where the dominant plants were conifers and cycads.

▲ The Jurassic period lasted from 208 m.y.a. to 145 m.y.a. During the Jurassic period, the supercontinent began to split apart, creating flooded rift valleys. Shallow oceans on the edges of the continent brought moister climates. Conifers, cycads, ferns, and horsetails flourished.

▲ The Cretaceous period lasted from 145 m.y.a. to 65 m.y.a. The Cretaceous saw the breakup of the supercontinent into smaller continents. Climates were warm and moist. Toward the end of the period, broadleaved forests and flowering plants evolved.

# Why dinosaurs died out

Dinosaurs ruled Earth for more than 165 million years, but then, 65 million years ago, they suddenly disappeared. No one is sure why this mass extinction took place, but there are many different theories. The most popular theory is that their death came from outer space when a comet or a massive piece of rock, called a meteorite, crashed to Earth.

▶ A huge comet or meteorite strike would have killed everything in the immediate area, caused forest fires, and sent tsunamis thundering across the oceans. The ash fallout could have lasted for hundreds of years. The main evidence for this catastrophic event is a buried crater on the Yucatán peninsula in Mexico that dates back to 65 million years ago.

### Extraterrestrial impact

Many geologists believe that at the end of the Cretaceous, Earth was hit by a comet or a 6-mi. (10-km)-wide meteorite. The impact created worldwide destruction, throwing up enough dust to block out the Sun for decades. As evidence for this theory, scientists have found something unusual in rocks dating from 65 million years ago—they contain 100 times more iridium than they should. Iridium is a metal that is rare on Earth's surface, but it is often found in space rocks.

exposed KT boundary

▲ Geologists look for clues about what happened at the end of the Cretaceous period in rocks from that time. The KT boundary is the dividing line between rocks laid down in the Cretaceous and rocks from the next period, the Tertiary. It has been well studied in the Badlands of South Dakota, where it has not been covered over by plants.

▲ Whatever killed the dinosaurs also made other life forms die out, including shellfish such as belemnites and this fossilized ammonite. Marine reptiles and pterosaurs disappeared. On land, every animal that was the size of a dog or larger became extinct.

▲ The dinosaurs may have become extinct at the end of the Cretaceous, but their descendants did not. These parrots are surviving theropods! All birds, from ducks to eagles, are direct descendants of the fierce meat eaters of the Mesozoic Era.

## Other theories

An alternative explanation for the extinction is that volcanoes sent up the dust that blocked out the Sun. Volcanic activity was certainly intense at that time—northwest India is made up of lava that erupted at the end of the Cretaceous period. This theory could also account for the iridium that was brought up from the depths of Earth. It is possible, of course, that both theories are correct. Perhaps the volcanoes were somehow triggered by the impact of a comet or meteor.

# SUMMARY OF CHAPTER 1: WORLD OF DINOSAURS

## What were the dinosaurs?

Dinosaurs were a group of ancient reptiles that were distinguished by having a number of their backbones fused together between their hips. They stood more like mammals than modern reptiles, with their legs swung beneath their bodies.

*Tyrannosaurus rex* skull

## Types of dinosaurs

The dinosaurs belonged to two groups. The first was the saurischians (lizard-hipped dinosaurs), which had their hipbones arranged like those of a lizard. The meat-eating theropods and the long-necked, plant-eating sauropods were both lizard-hipped. The second group was the ornithischians (bird-hipped dinosaurs), which had their hipbones arranged like those of a bird. All of the bird-hipped dinosaurs were plant eaters, with complex chewing mechanisms and beaks at the fronts of their mouths. Bird-hipped dinosaurs included the two-legged ornithopods and various types of armored dinosaurs.

## Evidence of dinosaurs

The dinosaurs were extremely successful and existed for more than 165 million years. They spread out over the whole world at a time when the geography of the globe was changing. When they first appeared, all of the landmasses were connected as one supercontinent. By the time that they disappeared, this had broken up into the individual continents that we know today. The dinosaurs all died out suddenly around 65 million years ago, probably as a result of a disaster such as a meteorite impact. We know about the dinosaurs because of fossils—their remains found in rocks that formed at the time. Dinosaur fossils are rare, so our knowledge about them appears in tiny trickles as new information appears.

# Go further . . .

 For general dinosaur information, go to: www.enchantedlearning.com/subjects/dinosaurs/

See some of the best dinosaur artwork today: dino.lm.com

For dinosaur descriptions, go to: www.dinodictionary.com

*1001 Facts About Dinosaurs* by Neil Clark, William Lindsay, and Dougal Dixon (Dorling Kindersley, 2002)

*The Kingfisher Illustrated Dinosaur Encyclopedia* by David Burnie (Kingfisher, 2001)

*The Illustrated Encyclopedia of Dinosaurs* by Dougal Dixon (Lorenz Books, 2006)

 **Climatologist**
Studies climates—the average weather conditions and temperature of a place over a long period of time.

**Geologist**
Studies the composition of Earth—the rocks and minerals that make it up, its history, and the processes that act upon it.

**Paleogeographer**
Studies what the world was like in the very distant past—the positions of the continents and the conditions that existed there.

**Paleontologist**
Studies the fossilized remains of creatures that lived long ago.

 Visit the American Museum of Natural History's famed dinosaurs' halls:
Central Park West at 79th Street
New York, NY 10024-5192
Phone: (212) 769-5100
www.amnh.org

See an 80-foot-tall *Diplodocus* skeleton at the Smithsonian:
National Museum of Natural History
P.O. Box 37012
Smithsonian Institute
Washington, D.C. 20013-7012
http://paleobiology.si.edu/dinosaurs//

*Psittacosaurus*, a dinosaur with a parrotlike head that lived in Asia during the Cretaceous period

## CHAPTER 2

# Eurasia

Europe is the birthplace of dinosaur discoveries. The first remains were found in England in the 1820s, and the name "dinosaur" was coined in 1842 by British anatomist Sir Richard Owen while he was reporting on a scientific meeting. In those days, the remains were merely scraps of bone and teeth. The 1878 discovery of several dozen *Iguanodon* skeletons, many complete, in a mine in Bernissart, Belgium, gave the world its first view of what a complete dinosaur looked like. In Asia, teams from the American Museum of Natural History in New York City made spectacular finds in Mongolia's Gobi desert, starting in the 1920s. More recently, in the last decade or so, there have been amazing discoveries in ancient lake deposits in Liaoning province, China. These have included perfect skeletons of tiny dinosaurs and early birds.

# The first dinosaur hunters

Imagine the thrill when people first discovered that giant reptiles, many times larger than elephants, had once roamed Earth. The realization came in the 1800s. Famous British fossil hunters included Mary Anning, William Buckland, and Gideon Mantell. Georges Cuvier was the foremost expert in France. Edward Cope and Othniel Marsh were important fossil hunters in the United States.

## Coining a name

English anatomist Richard Owen (1804–1892) studied many of the earliest fossil finds. To understand fossils, he looked at the anatomy of modern animals—he even dissected a rhinoceros in his own living room! In 1842 Owen came up with the name "Dinosauria" ("terrible lizards") to describe the group of extinct land reptiles.

## The big lizard

The first dinosaur species to be named was *Megalosaurus*, meaning "big lizard." British professor William Buckland (1784–1856) had found a fossil of its broken jaw in a quarry near Stonesfield, a short horse ride away from Oxford, England. Buckland presented the specimen at a scientific meeting in London on February 20, 1824.

▲ *Megalosaurus* fossils have been found in England, France, and Portugal, but never a whole skeleton. The fossilized jaw found by William Buckland showed new teeth growing up to replace old ones. As a meat eater, *Megalosaurus* may have lost teeth as it bit into prey.

**jawbone**

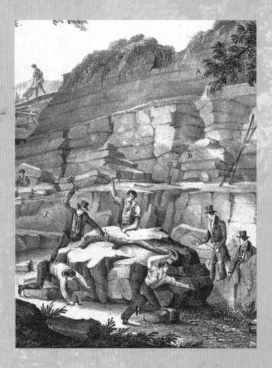

◄ Quarries were excellent searching grounds for early fossil hunters. In the early 1820s, an English doctor named Gideon Mantell (1790–1852) made a great discovery at this quarry close to Cuckfield in southern England. He and his wife, Mary, found fossilized bones and teeth belonging to the dinosaur *Iguanodon*.

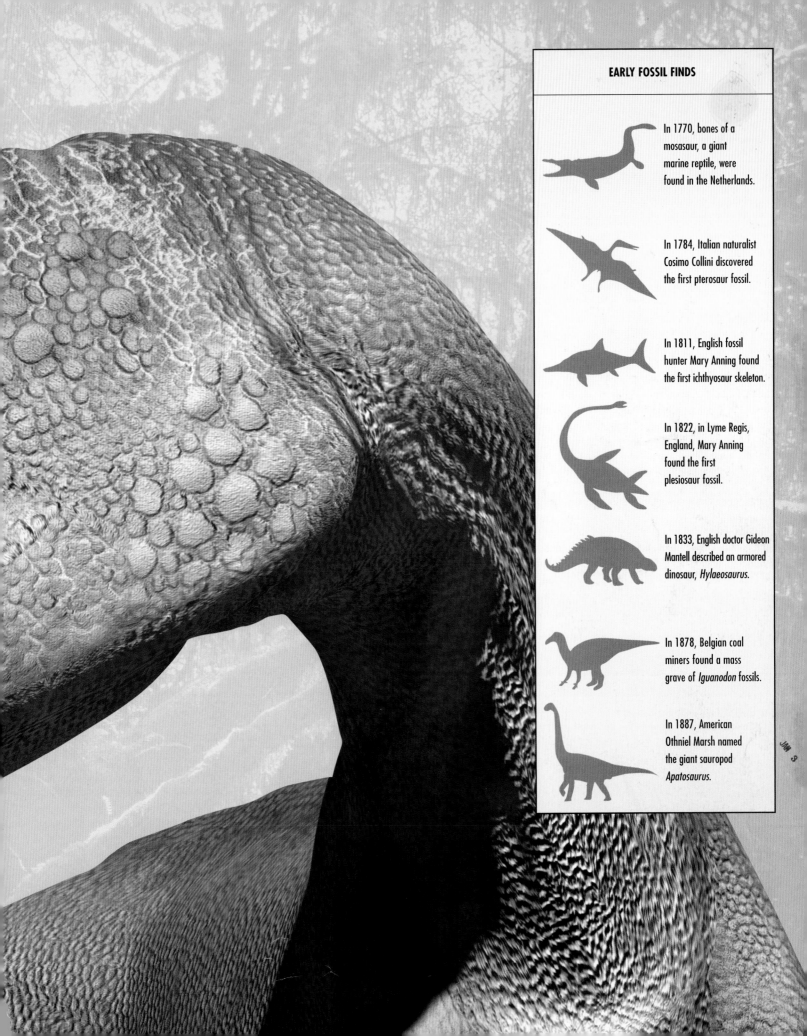

## EARLY FOSSIL FINDS

In 1770, bones of a mosasaur, a giant marine reptile, were found in the Netherlands.

In 1784, Italian naturalist Cosimo Collini discovered the first pterosaur fossil.

In 1811, English fossil hunter Mary Anning found the first ichthyosaur skeleton.

In 1822, in Lyme Regis, England, Mary Anning found the first plesiosaur fossil.

In 1833, English doctor Gideon Mantell described an armored dinosaur, *Hylaeosaurus*.

In 1878, Belgian coal miners found a mass grave of *Iguanodon* fossils.

In 1887, American Othniel Marsh named the giant sauropod *Apatosaurus*.

# The fossil record

Experts estimate that less than one percent of all dinosaurs were preserved as fossils. It is very rare for fossils to be found by accident. More often, they are discovered as a result of dedicated teamwork—and months of painstaking effort. But there is always an element of luck!

## Finding and mapping sites

In the early days of a dig, field geologists start prospecting—surveying for rocks that are likely to be rich in fossils. Once the site has been chosen, the hard work of clearing and digging begins. Most teams include student volunteers as well as professional scientists. Some team members may be responsible for running a field web site, uploading images and diaries.

## Excavating the fossils

Fossil bones are fragile. When they are still partly encased in rock, the paleontologists cover them with bandages dipped in plaster of Paris. This protects the bones from breaking. Back in the laboratory, the plaster "jacket" is cut away, revealing the fossil bit by bit. Microscopes and 3-D x-rays called CAT scans allow an even closer look.

▶ A 70-million-year-old fossil is uncovered in the Gobi desert in Mongolia. The original picture of the dig site has been altered here to show what the fossil eventually looked like after being cleaned and prepared in the laboratory. The bones belong to an *Oviraptor* that died defending its nest of 22 eggs.

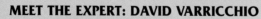

### MEET THE EXPERT: DAVID VARRICCHIO

American paleontologist David Varricchio visited a site in the Gobi desert in 2001. His job was to describe its geology. Rocks reveal what the entire environment was like millions of years ago and what event caused animals to be buried there.

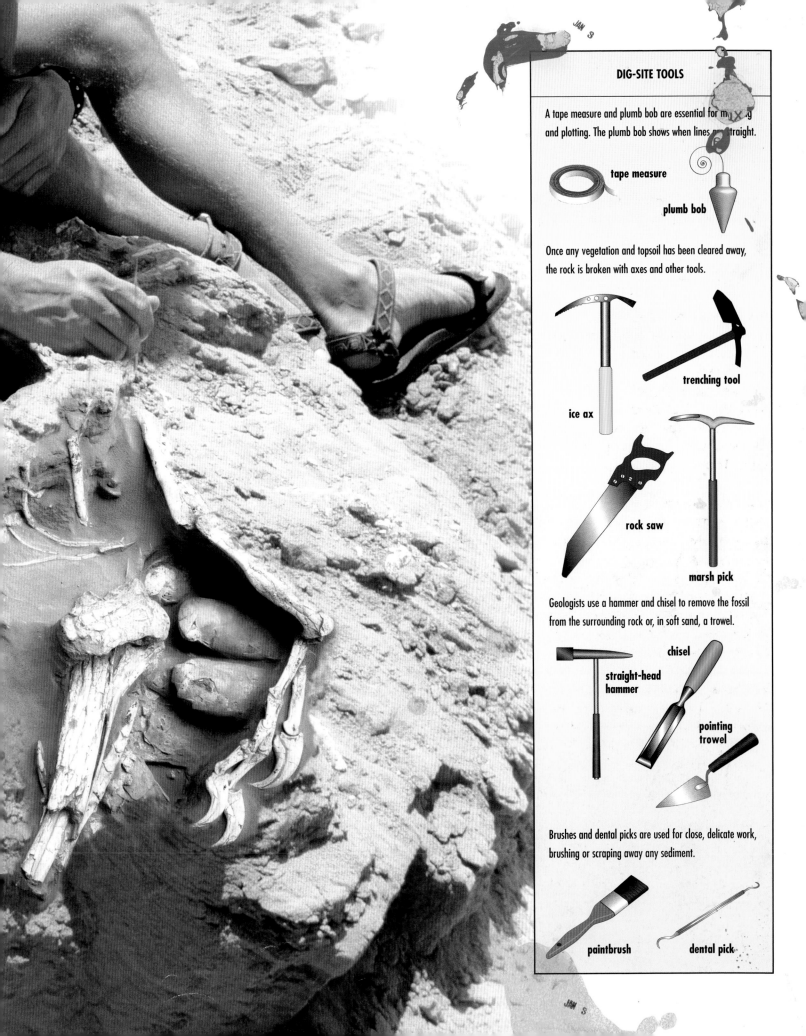

## DIG-SITE TOOLS

A tape measure and plumb bob are essential for m g and plotting. The plumb bob shows when lines traight.

**tape measure**

**plumb bob**

Once any vegetation and topsoil has been cleared away, the rock is broken with axes and other tools.

**trenching tool**

**ice ax**

**rock saw**

**marsh pick**

Geologists use a hammer and chisel to remove the fossil from the surrounding rock or, in soft sand, a trowel.

**chisel**

**straight-head hammer**

**pointing trowel**

Brushes and dental picks are used for close, delicate work, brushing or scraping away any sediment.

**paintbrush**

**dental pick**

# Fighting dinosaurs

The Gobi desert in Mongolia has been a rich source of fossils ever since the first *Protoceratops* skull was found there by Roy Chapman Andrews in 1922. A fossil known as the "fighting dinosaurs" was discovered there in 1971. It shows a *Protoceratops* and *Velociraptor* locked in a fight to the death. They were buried alive 80 million years ago during a landslide.

### Victim and attacker

*Protoceratops* was a plant eater that had a bony shield to protect its neck. Although it belonged to the ceratopsian (horned dinosaur) family, it did not have horns—just bony lumps and bumps on its face. Its main defense was running away, and it had broad, hooflike claws that could dig into the sandy ground. *Velociraptor* was the chief enemy of *Protoceratops*. This predator had slender but powerful jaws that contained long rows of bladed teeth. It also had huge claws, which it used to grip its prey.

▶ The Mongolian dinosaurs were fairly small—the meat eaters were around the size of large dogs, and the herbivores were the size of sheep. *Protoceratops* was so common that it is sometimes called "the sheep of the Cretaceous."

## MEET THE EXPERT: MARK NORELL

Mark Norell of the American Museum of Natural History in New York City has a special interest in the "fighting dinosaurs" fossil. In 2000, he commissioned computer animators to bring the dinosaur duel to life for a special exhibition of the fossil. He has also worked to show how theropods, such as *Velociraptor*, had feathers, not scales.

◀ This animatronic model of a feathered *Velociraptor* was built for London's Natural History Museum. Plumage would have kept in body heat—essential for an active, warm-blooded hunter. The feathers may have been brightly colored for display or dull for camouflage. They definitely were not used for flying.

**Velociraptor**

**Protoceratops**

▲ The famous "fighting dinosaurs" fossil captures two dinosaurs in an embrace of death. The *Velociraptor* has grasped its victim's head in its clawed hands and embedded its feet deep into the plant eater's stomach. *Protoceratops* is fighting back, snapping its enemy's arm tightly in its beak.

## Gobi treasure trove

American fossil hunter Roy Chapman Andrews (1884–1960) described his 1922 fossil hunt to the Gobi desert as "the biggest land scientific expedition ever to leave the United States." His extraordinary finds included skeletons of adult and juvenile *Protoceratops*, as well as the *Velociraptor*s that preyed upon them. Later expeditions to the area uncovered hundreds of dinosaur eggs. Some had been laid by *Protoceratops*, while others belonged to *Oviraptor*. The name *Oviraptor* means "egg thief." When *Oviraptor* was first discovered, paleontologists did not know that all dinosaurs laid eggs. They thought that *Oviraptor* must have stolen the eggs of *Protoceratops*.

# Feathered dinosaurs

Paleontologist Xu Xing has found more than 25 dinosaurs and discovered a great deal of evidence that birds are dinosaurs. His spectacular specimens include small meat-eating dinosaurs with feathers, not scales. Xing works in Liaoning province, China. Around 130 million years ago, volcanic eruptions in the region preserved Early Cretaceous animals in a layer of ash.

Until the 1990s, all dinosaurs were thought to have scaly, reptilian skin. The only question was what color the skin was, since fossilization does not preserve color. Then, in 1995, the first feathered dinosaur, *Sinosauropteryx*, was discovered in China. Feathers may have first appeared when reptile scales frayed at the edges and became downy fluff, which kept dinosaurs warm. Later, fluff evolved into feathers, possibly for display.

▶ A pair of *Microraptors* flash their feathers, perhaps to fight for territory or to attract mates. *Microraptor* was around the size of a crow and probably not capable of powered flight. However, it could have spread its wings to glide from tree to tree.

▲ The very fine fossil of *Microraptor* clearly shows feathers fanning out from the arms and legs. These limbs evidently formed two pairs of wings. The feathered tail would have provided steering as *Microraptor* glided through Cretaceous skies.

**Wings outstretched for gliding**

**Showy tail feathers**

**Downy body covering**

## How flight began

Most paleontologists agree that birds evolved from dinosaurs. However, they do not agree about how flight evolved. Some believe that it was a "trees-down" process, in which a climbing animal learned to glide from branch to branch. This helped it move from tree to tree. Others believe in a "ground-up" process, in which a running and jumping animal evolved wings that helped it run faster and jump higher—so that it could be better at hunting insects and other small, speedy prey.

## From dromaeosaurs to birds

The fast little hunters called dromaeosaurs were the most birdlike of the dinosaurs. Their limbs were hollow, and they were probably warm-blooded and covered in feathers for insulation. They are birds' closest relatives. However, they appeared later than the first birds, showing that the evolutionary line is very complex. It has even been suggested that dromaeosaurs were actually early birds that had lost their powers of flight!

### FEATHERED DINOSAURS

*Sinosauropteryx* was very similar to the tiny *Compsognathus*, but it was covered in a fine covering of downy feathers. It must have had an active lifestyle.

*Protarchaeopteryx* had bunches of long feathers on its tail and wings. Despite its "wings," *Protarchaeopteryx* could not fly.

*Mei* was found curled up like a sleeping duck, with its head tucked under its arm. Its full scientific name—*Mei long*—means "sleeping dragon."

# Flying reptiles

Pterosaurs, the first backboned creatures to fly, appeared in the Late Triassic period and soared over the heads of the dinosaurs. From the Late Jurassic, they shared the skies with early birds. Pterosaurs had a variety of feeding techniques. Some snapped up insects in midair, others swooped down to scoop up fish, and some may have even scavenged dinosaur carcasses.

### Little and large

Pterosaurs came in many shapes and sizes. The earliest ones had long tails, but the pterodactyls, which came later, had short, stumpy tails. Some pterosaurs were barely bigger than blackbirds, while others were the size of small aircraft. Unlike birds, whose wings are made of feathers, pterosaurs had wings made of living tissue, containing a network of blood vessels. Pterosaurs were warm-blooded and had a fine covering of hair to conserve their body heat.

◄ Gliding reptiles appeared more than 260 m.y.a.—long before the pterosaurs—but they could not stay airborne for long. *Xianglong*, a gliding lizard that lived 125 m.y.a., looked a lot like this modern *Draco* lizard from Southeast Asia.

► This Late Jurassic scene shows pterosaurs flying, feeding, and nesting. The best pterosaur fossils are of species that lived close to water. This is because their remains ended up on the seabed and, over time, became preserved as sedimentary rock formed.

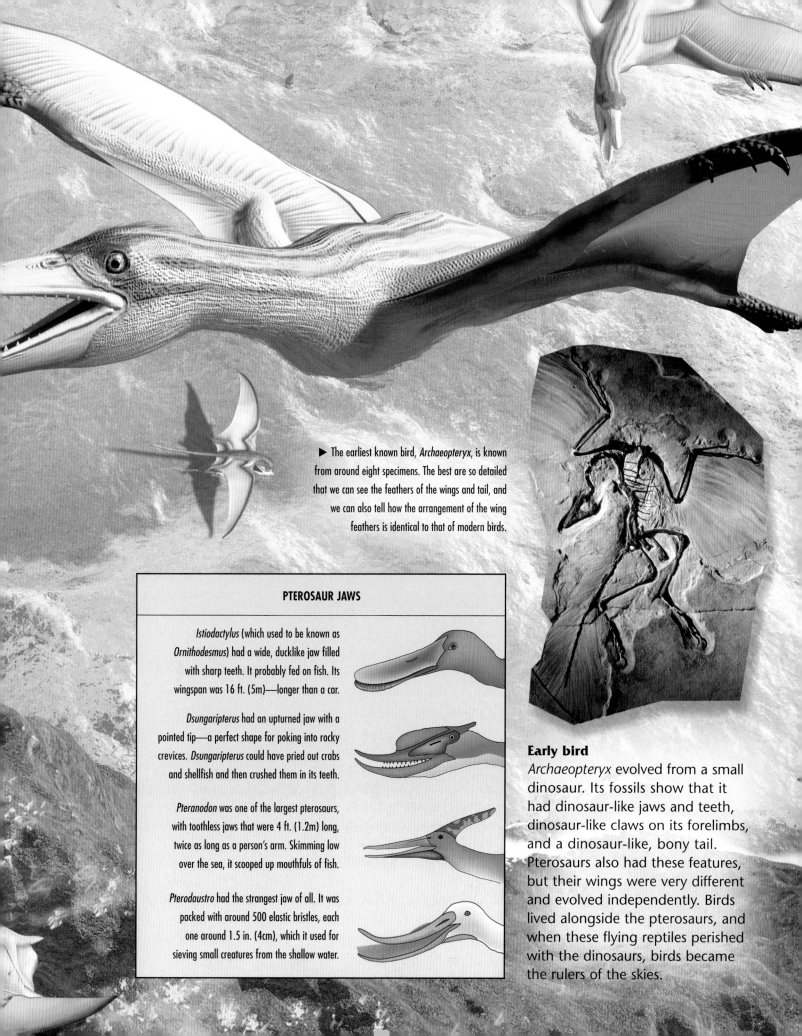

▶ The earliest known bird, *Archaeopteryx*, is known from around eight specimens. The best are so detailed that we can see the feathers of the wings and tail, and we can also tell how the arrangement of the wing feathers is identical to that of modern birds.

## PTEROSAUR JAWS

*Istiodactylus* (which used to be known as *Ornithodesmus*) had a wide, ducklike jaw filled with sharp teeth. It probably fed on fish. Its wingspan was 16 ft. (5m)—longer than a car.

*Dsungaripterus* had an upturned jaw with a pointed tip—a perfect shape for poking into rocky crevices. *Dsungaripterus* could have pried out crabs and shellfish and then crushed them in its teeth.

*Pteranodon* was one of the largest pterosaurs, with toothless jaws that were 4 ft. (1.2m) long, twice as long as a person's arm. Skimming low over the sea, it scooped up mouthfuls of fish.

*Pterodaustro* had the strangest jaw of all. It was packed with around 500 elastic bristles, each one around 1.5 in. (4cm), which it used for sieving small creatures from the shallow water.

### Early bird

*Archaeopteryx* evolved from a small dinosaur. Its fossils show that it had dinosaur-like jaws and teeth, dinosaur-like claws on its forelimbs, and a dinosaur-like, bony tail. Pterosaurs also had these features, but their wings were very different and evolved independently. Birds lived alongside the pterosaurs, and when these flying reptiles perished with the dinosaurs, birds became the rulers of the skies.

# Marine reptiles

Before anyone knew about dinosaurs, the study of ancient marine reptiles was well under way. Fossils of sea animals are much more common than those of land animals. This is because most fossils are preserved in sedimentary rock, which forms when sediment piles up at the bottom of the sea. In the late 1700s and early 1800s, geologists and anatomists were studying the strange animals that swam in the ancient oceans.

---

## MARINE REPTILE GROUPS

Nothosaurs (245–228 m.y.a.) had webbed feet or flippers. They hunted in shallow coastal waters.

Pliosaurs (200–65 m.y.a.) had compact bodies, short necks, massive heads, and ferocious jaws.

Mosasaurs (140–65 m.y.a.) swam by rippling their bodies, using their flippers only for steering and stability.

Ichthyosaurs (247–140 m.y.a.) had four flippers, crescent-shaped tails, and streamlined, dolphinlike bodies.

Plesiosaurs (200–65 m.y.a.) had four broad flippers, or paddles. They swung their necks through schools of fish.

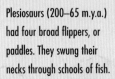

Shelled reptiles included placodonts (240–200 m.y.a.) and turtles (215 m.y.a. to the present day).

Baby ichthyosaur being born

▲ Ichthyosaurs were superbly adapted for life in the ocean. Unlike other marine reptiles, they did not come ashore to lay eggs. Instead, they had live young in the ocean. This *Ichthyosaurus* specimen was fossilized during the act of giving birth.

▲ *Plesiosaurus* used its large paddles to power through the water after prey. It waved its long, flexible neck this way and that, picking off fish from a school. *Plesiosaurus* only grew to around 10 ft. (3m), but one of its relatives, *Elasmosaurus*, grew as long as 46 ft. (14m).

## Underwater flight

Plesiosaurs and their short-necked, big-headed relatives the pliosaurs swam through the water in a kind of flying motion. The legs had evolved into stiff paddles, reinforced by a mosaic of bones that had once formed fingers and wrists. These paddles worked like the wings of a bird. By flapping them slowly up and down, the animal moved forward. Modern-day turtles, penguins, and sea lions move through the water in a similar way.

## Swimming and hunting

Ichthyosaurs and mosasaurs swam with a rippling motion of the body and tail, using their paddlelike legs for steering. Mosasaurs were like giant swimming lizards—the largest grew to 56 ft. (17m). They ate just about anything, from ammonites to sharks and plesiosaurs. Ichthyosaurs fed on squidlike shellfish called belemnites. Some had eyes as large as dinner plates so that they could dive to deep, dark depths in search of prey.

# SUMMARY OF CHAPTER 2: EURASIA

### Early studies
Europe is where the systematic study of fossil vertebrates (backboned animals) first started. In the late 1700s and early 1800s, the bones of mosasaurs, plesiosaurs, and ichthyosaurs were being recognized for what they were—the remains of ancient animals. These prehistoric marine reptiles were collected and studied scientifically. In dinosaur times, most of Europe was covered in shallow oceans, in which these animals lived.

### Land reptiles
The study expanded to include ancient land reptiles following three key discoveries—William Buckland's *Megalosaurus*, found in 1822, and the two specimens identified by Gideon Mantell: *Iguanodon*, found in 1825, and the armored *Hylaeosaurus*, found in 1832. Richard Owen established the classification (biological group) of "Dinosauria" to accommodate these three new animals.

### The science spreads
In the 1900s and 2000s there have been finds all across Europe and Asia. The Cretaceous rocks of the Gobi desert have been studied since the 1920s. There scientists have found the fossils of early horned dinosaurs and small, fast meat eaters. Fossilized dinosaur eggs have also been found in the Gobi desert, along with the parents that died trying to hatch them. Farther east, in China, there are ancient lake deposits that have fossils of early birds and tiny feathered dinosaurs. The smallest dinosaurs that ever lived are being discovered there.

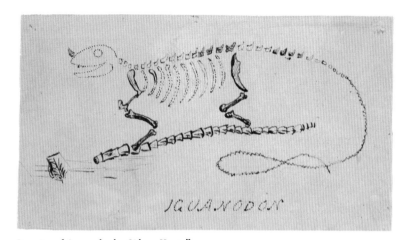
Drawing of *Iguanodon* by Gideon Mantell

# Go further . . .

Discover some of the best TV shows about dinosaurs at: www.bbc.co.uk/sn/prehistoric_life

Read a thorough overview on the subject of dinosaurs at: www.ucmp.berkeley.edu/diapsids/dinosaur.html

Read about Gideon Mantell and his discovery of *Iguanodon* at: www.strangescience.net/mantell.htm

*Dinosaur Quest* by Steve Parker and John Sibbick (Cornwall Editions Limited, 2005)

*Feathered Dinosaurs of China* by Gregory C. Wenzel (Charlesbridge Publishing, 2004)

**Anatomist**
Studies how animals are built and what the different parts of their bodies are used for.

**Field geologist**
Works on rock outcrops ("out in the field") instead of just studying rocks in a laboratory.

**Naturalist**
Studies nature and living things, especially animals and plants.

**Ornithologist**
Studies birds. Some ornithologists observe birds out in the wild or use technologies, such as radar, to track bird populations. Others study bird anatomy in the laboratory.

Observe two Jurassic supergiants, *Seismosaurus* and *Saurophaganax*, fight to the death at the New Mexico Museum of Natural History and Science:
1801 Mountain Road NW
Albuquerque, NM 87014
Phone: (505) 841-2800
www.nmnaturalhistory.org

"Feathered Dinosaurs of China" is a traveling exhibit that has been touring many museums worldwide since 2002. Check it out if it comes to your local area.

## CHAPTER 3

# The Americas

After Europe, North America was the next place for dinosaur discoveries. In the second half of the 1800s, dinosaur hunters moved west, finding fossilized bones as they went. Two professors—Othniel Marsh of Yale University in Connecticut and Edward Cope of the University of Pennsylvania—became bitter rivals as they tried to outdo each other in the number of their finds. "Dinomania" spread. Around 150 types of dinosaurs had been discovered by 1900. Canada became the next important hunting area, with dinosaurs even being found as far north as Alaska. Starting in the 1970s, South America became a dinosaur hunter's paradise. The vast plains of Argentina have given us all types of dinosaurs and even nesting sites, while areas of Brazil are now famous for their pterosaurs and fish-eating dinosaurs.

Exposed sauropod backbones on the quarry wall at Dinosaur National Monument in Utah

# Hunting in packs

During the Cretaceous period, North America was home to some terrifying predators. Dromaeosaurs, such as *Dromaeosaurus* and *Deinonychus*, were intelligent and fast-moving, often working together in packs to bring down creatures that were much larger than themselves. They shared their habitat with other clever hunters, such as *Troodon* and the ornithomimids ("bird mimics").

## Killing machine

Imagine a hunting dinosaur the size of a wolf. Give it long hind legs and the running speed of a greyhound. Equip each foot with a huge, curved claw that could hook into flesh. Make it as intelligent as a bird of prey. You have imagined a dromaeosaur.

▲ A pack of wolf-size *Deinonychus* attacks a *Tenontosaurus*. Curved claws on their fingers and an enormous, sickle-shaped claw on their second toe allow them to hook onto their victim. They bite and bite again, slashing the *Tenontosaurus* with razor-sharp teeth until it finally collapses from loss of blood.

▲ Like the dromaeosaurs, *Troodon* was armed with lethal claws. It also had a fairly large brain, making it one of the smartest dinosaurs around. It had large eyes, so it possibly hunted at dusk or at night.

## MEET THE EXPERT: PHIL MANNING

Paleontologist Phil Manning demonstrated that dromaeosaurs could not have used their outsize claws to kill. He attached a life-size *Deinonychus* claw to a robotic arm and thrust it into a slab of meat. It did not go in deeply enough to have caused fatal wounds. Manning realized that the claws were not for wounding, but for hooking onto prey before biting it to death.

## The gentle relative

The ornithomimids were a group of fast-running dinosaurs. The name, meaning "bird mimic," comes from their resemblance to modern ostriches. Ornithomimids used their speed to escape rather than to hunt. Instead of jaws full of deadly teeth, they had toothless beaks. Bird mimics probably fed on small animals such as lizards, rodents, and insects. Some of them may even have been fruit eaters.

◄ *Struthiomimus* (the "ostrich mimic") was one of the ornithomimids. Its muscular legs helped carry it away from dangerous dromaeosaurs. It had a short, light tail and could run at speeds of 30 mph (50km/h)—as fast as a racehorse.

# Armored dinosaurs

Early plant eaters relied on size to protect them from predators. Later, some herbivores evolved body armor. Ceratopsians, or horned dinosaurs, were the tanks of the dinosaur world. Like rhinos today, they had fearsome horns. Nodosaurs and ankylosaurs had all-over armor, with horns, bony plates, and, sometimes, a tail weapon.

## Horned dinosaurs

Ceratopsians lived across the Northern Hemisphere. *Triceratops*, *Styracosaurus*, and *Centrosaurus* inhabited what is now North America. Many of these plant eaters had powerful beaks that could snap through branches. However, their main features were their formidable horns, which projected from bony skull shields and were edged with a frill of spikes. The biggest ceratopsians were a match for any predator, including *Tyrannosaurus rex*.

## Bony armor and plates

The armored dinosaurs were common at the end of the Cretaceous period, mostly on the northern continents, although one fossil has been found in Australia. There were two types. The first were the nodosaurs, which had armored backs and spikes along the sides, especially on the shoulders. The ankylosaurs had no side spikes but had a bony club on the end of their tail.

▲ *Euoplocephalus* was a typical armored ankylosaur. Even its eyelids were armored—they protected the eyes like steel shutters. *Euoplocephalus* had a tail club, too, for striking back at predators.

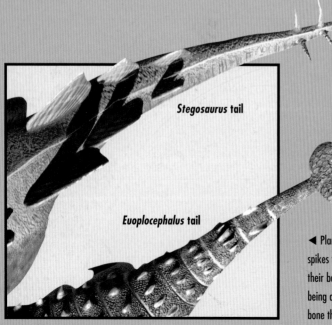

*Stegosaurus* tail

*Euoplocephalus* tail

◄ Plant eaters' tails were powerful weapons. Stegosaurs had tail spikes to stab attackers. They also had bony plates or spines along their backs, but these were probably used for heat loss rather than being a form of armor. *Euoplocephalus* had a clublike knob of bone that could break a predator's leg with a single swipe.

▶ This fossilized skull belongs to *Triceratops*. Like all ceratopsians, it had a heavy head and an armored shield around its neck. In some species, this shield was ringed with spikes. *Triceratops* had three horns on its head. Other ceratopsians had two, one, or even none.

# Famous giants

Patagonia, in Argentina, is a hot spot for dinosaur bones. For tens of millions of years, the region was a humid swamp inhabited by dinosaurs. Around 130 million years ago it was home to *Amargasaurus*, a 30-ft. (9-m)-long beast with forked spines down its back. From 100 to 80 million years ago, Patagonia was a land of giants. Herds of colossal *Argentinosaurus* were stalked by terrifying predators, which were possibly bigger than *Tyrannosaurus rex*.

### Giant sauropod

*Argentinosaurus* ("Argentina lizard") was possibly the largest, heaviest land animal that has ever lived. From the bones that they have, experts estimate that *Argentinosaurus* was 115 ft. (35m) long and weighed more than 15 elephants. It was one of the specialized sauropods that survived on the island continent of South America even after sauropods had begun to disappear elsewhere. Cretaceous South America had been isolated for so long that animals continued to evolve there that were found nowhere else.

▲ With average rainfall of around 51 in. (130mm) per year, Patagonia has an extremely dry climate. There is very little vegetation, so rocks lie exposed in the dusty desert. Any fossils contained within the rocks, such as this dinosaur spine, are easily seen.

▲ The middle vertebra (backbone segment) in this picture belonged to *Argentinosaurus*, while the two on both sides came from smaller sauropods. The wide parts of the bones anchored powerful muscles and cablelike ligaments (bundles of tissue). While it was alive, these were needed to support and power the huge body.

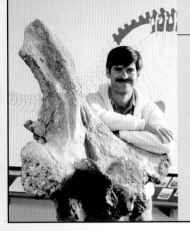

### MEET THE EXPERT: RODOLFO CORIA

When a car mechanic and a farmer reported finding huge bones in Patagonia to the local museum in Plaza Huincul, resident paleontologist Rodolfo Coria investigated. He excavated both sites and named the owners of the bones *Giganotosaurus* and *Argentinosaurus* respectively.

## Giant theropod

For decades we regarded *Tyrannosaurus rex* as the largest, fiercest dinosaur that ever lived. Today, however, we are finding the remains of even bigger meat eaters, such as *Giganotosaurus* from the Middle Cretaceous period of South America. Like all theropods, *Giganotosaurus* had a huge head, sharp teeth, and clawed hands that it held out at the front, balanced by a heavy tail. It probably preyed on the huge sauropods of the time. It was more closely related to the earlier allosaurs than the later tyrannosaurs.

▼ A *Giganotosaurus* brings down a young *Argentinosaurus*. To take on an adult sauropod, *Giganotosaurus* had to work as part of a team. In this reconstruction, *Buitreraptors* lurk in the background, ready to dart in for scraps of meat. These scavengers behaved like jackals at a lion kill today.

# Hell Creek today

Hell Creek—what an exciting-sounding name! For paleontologists, this bleak badland area in the remote northwest of the United States more than lives up to its name. Sixty-five million years ago it was the stomping ground of *Tyrannosaurus rex*, *Triceratops*, and many other famous dinosaurs. Today, its rocks are revealing some of the most impressive dinosaur fossils that have ever been found.

▲ Tracks discovered by Phil Manning in the Hell Creek rocks may show the first known footprints of *Tyrannosaurus*. The shape and the size are right, and *Tyrannosaurus* lived in the area at that time. However, without any other evidence, ichnologists (fossil footprint experts) cannot definitely say what made the tracks.

### Hell's inhabitants

The sandstones of Hell Creek were deposited in rivers and swamps over a period of two million years at the very end of the Cretaceous period. There are fossils of laurels, magnolias, and conifers—the remains of ancient forests. Among these plant fossils, paleontologists are finding the bones of duck-billed dinosaurs and ceratopsians. There is also evidence of small meat eaters, such as dromaeosaurs and *Troodon*, as well as the mighty *Tyrannosaurus rex*.

▼ A fossil hunter walks through the dusty Dakota Badlands. Over many thousands of years, wind, rain, and ice have worn away the landscape. The weathering has exposed layers of Hell Creek Formation rock, which are rich in dinosaur fossils.

Crooked Creek Formation

Fort Peck Lake

Hell Creek Bay

Peterson Point

Hell Creek Formation

North America

M O N T A N A

▲ The Hell Creek Formation is named after exposed sections of Cretaceous rock that run along Hell Creek in Montana. However, the rock formation—and its prehistoric treasure— is spread over parts of North and South Dakota, too.

▲ One of the most exciting Hell Creek discoveries was a *Thescelosaurus* nicknamed "Willow." Remains of this cow-size herbivore had been found before, but Willow was special because preserved inside its chest were the remains of a structure that some have interpreted as a heart (see page 45).

## Tyrant king

*Tyrannosaurus rex* had a massive skull, with teeth and jaws that were powerful enough to crush bone. Its eyes were able to focus forward on its prey. Its body weighed as much as an elephant, but this terrifying meat eater was still able to race along on its mighty hind legs. What a monster! No wonder scientists gave it a name that means "king of the tyrant reptiles."

◄ More than 50 *Tyrannosaurus* specimens have been discovered since the first one was found in 1905. The skeleton shown here is one of the most complete *Tyrannosauruses*. It was nicknamed "Stan" after its finder, Stan Sacrison. It is now mounted in the Black Hills Museum in Hill City, South Dakota.

# Hell Creek long ago

Imagine dinosaurs lumbering through the Everglades, a 21st-century swamp in southern Florida, and you'll get a good idea of what prehistoric Hell Creek was like. The climate was hot, damp, and perfect for dinosaurs. There were many types of insects, including dragonflies and blood-sucking mosquitoes. The dinosaurs there would also have heard bird calls, just as we do today.

**Animals of Hell Creek**
With its lush, forested riverbanks and steamy swamps, Hell Creek had a thriving ecosystem 65 million years ago. The forest trees and undergrowth were browsed by plant-eating dinosaurs such as ceratopsians and duckbills. These, in turn, were hunted by the big meat eaters. Smaller animals, such as turtles and birds, were hunted by the smaller meat-eating dinosaurs and by crocodiles.

**Vegetation at Hell Creek**
Plant life was changing during the Late Cretaceous. There were still many conifers, but the ancient cycads and ginkgoes were on the way out. A new group of plants was taking over—plants with flowers. Vegetation was no longer just green. Flowers had color in order to attract pollinating insects. Grasses did not evolve until after the extinction of the dinosaurs, but the Hell Creek landscape may have included some types of trees that are still around today such as birch, beech, fig, palm, oak, and willow.

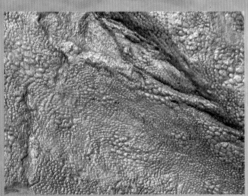

▲ This specimen of fossilized skin, found in Wyoming, belonged to *Edmontosaurus*, one of the largest hadrosaurs. It shows that the dinosaur had raised nodules on its skin. Fossilized skin is rare. It formed only when hot, dry conditions mummified a dead dinosaur and prevented its soft tissues from rotting.

# Hadrosaurs

With flattened snouts that resembled ducks' beaks, hadrosaurs are sometimes nicknamed duck-billed dinosaurs. They were midsize dinosaurs, between 20–59 ft. (6m–18m) long, and they usually lived in herds. They are most famous for their flamboyant heads, since many hadrosaurs had hollow crests in unusual shapes. Their jaws were distinctive too, containing multiple rows of hundreds of teeth for chewing tough vegetation.

▼ *Parasaurolophus* had a crest up to 6 ft. (1.8m) long—the most impressive of any hadrosaur. Here, a *Parasaurolophus* group comes to the river to drink, unaware that a 49-ft. (15-m)-long crocodile, *Deinosuchus*, is lying in wait to ambush one of them.

▶ This is a model *Maiasaura* nest. The real thing consisted of a mound of soil, around 3 ft. (1m) high and 6.5 ft. (2m) wide, with a hollow in the top. *Maiasaura* herds nested together, with each nest within pecking distance of the next.

## Good mothers

In the 1970s, paleontologist Jack Horner found a nesting site in Montana belonging to a new species of hadrosaur. Horner called the 30-ft. (10-m)-long creature *Maiasaura* ("good mother lizard") because it seemed that the parents cared for their young, feeding them berries, seeds, and leaves. Some nests had newly-hatched babies, only 19.5 in. (50cm) long, while others contained older ones as long as 6.5 ft. (2m).

## Making music

The duckbill's crest was probably used for making a noise. A long, tubular crest like that of *Parasaurolophus* would have made a noise like a trombone. Smaller crests created different sounds. The calls were used for communication and keeping the herd together.

# Titanosaur nursery

In 1997 an extraordinary nesting site was discovered in Patagonia, Argentina. From the fossilized remains, we can imagine the scene 80 million years ago. Female *Saltasaurus* dinosaurs, each weighing seven tons, gathered on a floodplain to lay their eggs. Each female dug a shallow nest, flicking sand and soil into the air, and then dropped in its eggs with a soft plop. After laying as many as 30 eggs, the female covered the nest with soil and left the eggs to be hatched by the warmth of the sun.

▲ There is no evidence that any adult *Saltasaurus* remained to guard the nesting site. Most eggs and hatchlings would have been eaten by predatory *Aucasaurus* dinosaurs. Hatchlings would have begun feeding immediately—it would take 15 or 20 years for them to reach their adult size.

### MEET THE EXPERT: LUIS CHIAPPÉ

Argentinian paleontologist Luis Chiappé led the team that discovered the *Saltasaurus* nursery. He was looking for fossilized birds, not dinosaur eggs! Instead, Chiappé stumbled upon the world's biggest dinosaur nesting site and the first-ever discovery of sauropod embryos. The site was in a region of Patagonia called Auca Mahuida. Chiappé's team renamed it "Auca Mahuevo," playing on the Spanish word *huevo*, meaning "egg."

## Regular nesting

We cannot tell how often the *Saltasaurus* herds visited Auca Mahuevo or for how long the nesting site was in operation. However, the thickness of the sediments suggest that it was probably a regular nesting area for hundreds of years.

## Dead eggs

We know about the nesting site because once in a while it was flooded by a nearby river. This buried the eggs in mud, and they fossilized. Most of the time, however, this did not happen, and the eggs that were not eaten hatched safely. The youngsters left the site and the eggshells rotted away, leaving no sign that they had ever been there.

▶ Each *Saltasaurus* egg was only 4.7 in. (12cm) across, slightly smaller than an ostrich egg. Amazingly, the embryo inside would eventually grow into an adult titanosaur as long as two buses!

# Warm- or cold-blooded?

For a long time, paleontologists thought that dinosaurs were cold-blooded, like modern reptiles. Cold-blooded animals cannot produce their own heat. Their temperature changes depending on their surroundings. However, since the late 1960s, some paleontologists have argued that dinosaurs could have been warm-blooded, like mammals and birds today. Warm-blooded animals are able to keep their bodies at a constant temperature.

▼ A constant body temperature would have been useful to a speedy hunter such as this *Bambiraptor*. If *Bambiraptor* was warm-blooded, it would have needed an efficient, chambered heart to pump blood upward to its head.

## Cold-blooded reptiles

A cold-blooded animal's metabolism (how it makes energy from food) requires less food than a warm-blooded animal's does. So a cold-blooded dinosaur would have hunted in violent spurts of activity, with long rests in between. Some experts say that a big meat eater, such as *Tyrannosaurus rex*, would never have been able to hunt enough food if it was warm-blooded, so it must have been cold-blooded.

◄ One theory suggests that the biggest dinosaurs, such as *Diplodocus*, were so massive that they held onto their warmth, instead of cooling down as the weather got cooler. This is known as being gigantothermic. By retaining heat, they could have had a warm-blooded lifestyle without needing a warm-blooded metabolism.

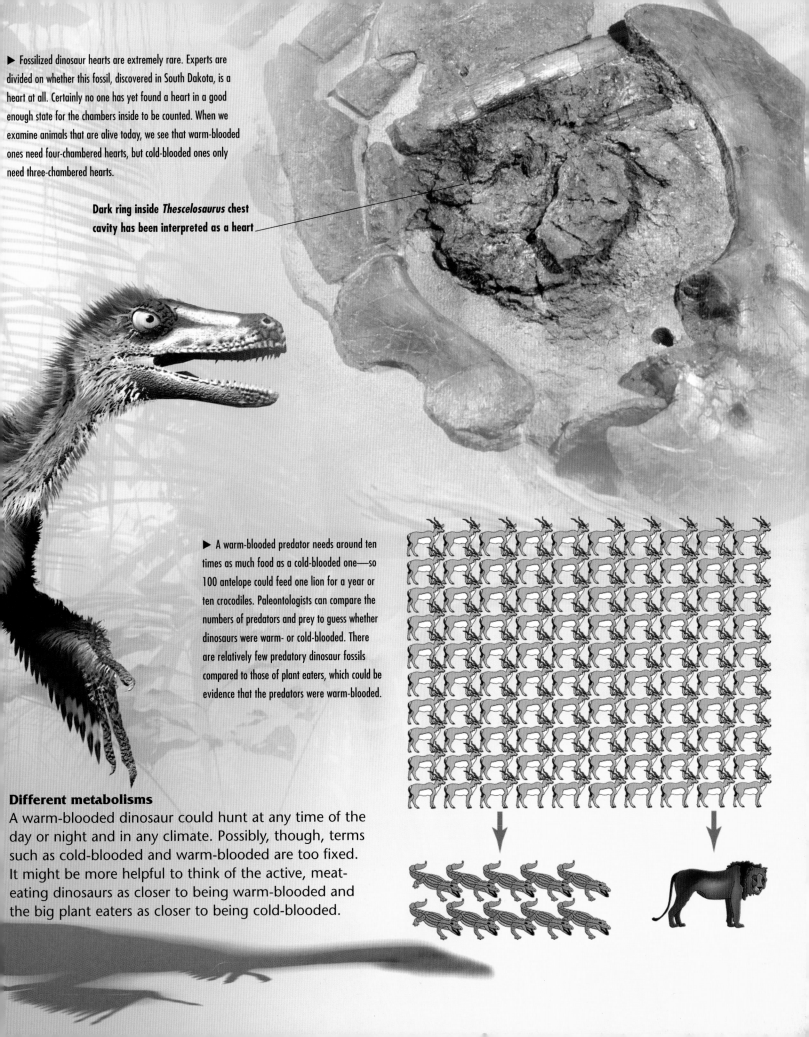

► Fossilized dinosaur hearts are extremely rare. Experts are divided on whether this fossil, discovered in South Dakota, is a heart at all. Certainly no one has yet found a heart in a good enough state for the chambers inside to be counted. When we examine animals that are alive today, we see that warm-blooded ones need four-chambered hearts, but cold-blooded ones only need three-chambered hearts.

Dark ring inside *Thescelosaurus* chest cavity has been interpreted as a heart

► A warm-blooded predator needs around ten times as much food as a cold-blooded one—so 100 antelope could feed one lion for a year or ten crocodiles. Paleontologists can compare the numbers of predators and prey to guess whether dinosaurs were warm- or cold-blooded. There are relatively few predatory dinosaur fossils compared to those of plant eaters, which could be evidence that the predators were warm-blooded.

## Different metabolisms

A warm-blooded dinosaur could hunt at any time of the day or night and in any climate. Possibly, though, terms such as cold-blooded and warm-blooded are too fixed. It might be more helpful to think of the active, meat-eating dinosaurs as closer to being warm-blooded and the big plant eaters as closer to being cold-blooded.

# SUMMARY OF CHAPTER 3: THE AMERICAS

## Dinosaur societies

The finds of North and South America have given us plenty of insight into dinosaur social life over the years, with dinosaur nests and young found in Montana and in Patagonia, Argentina. Fossils of herds have shown that duckbills of North America moved around in herds and family groups. We have also found out that some of the more active meat eaters hunted in packs like wolves.

## Sharing the landscape

The first finds in North America showed how all types of dinosaurs lived together in one place. Big, plant-eating sauropods, such as *Apatasaurus* and *Argentinosaurus*, browsed the higher vegetation. Smaller ornithopods, including

*Allosaurus* skeleton

the duckbills, ate the lower-growing plants. Large meat eaters, such as *Allosaurus, Giganotosaurus*, and *Tyrannosaurus*, lived by hunting other animals. The remains from the end of the age of dinosaurs show the spectacular development of horned and armored dinosaurs. Horns and armor against teeth and claws—it was an arms race!

## Different then from now

The modern-day sites that show the best dinosaur fossils are completely different from what they were like in dinosaur times. The Hell Creek area of the United States and the Patagonia region of Argentina are now arid badlands, with no large animals living there at all. In the Cretaceous period, these regions had forests and rivers and were populated by herds of huge dinosaurs.

## Heart of the dinosaurs

Despite the find of a possible *Thescelosaurus* heart in Hell Creek, there is still a debate as to whether dinosaurs were cold-blooded, warm-blooded, or something in between. Future fossil finds may help solve this mystery.

# Go further . . .

Hunt dinosaurs in the desert: www.desertusa.com/mag98/dec/stories/dinosafari.html

Read about the 19th-century "bone wars": www.levins.com/bwars.shtml

Read an interview with Luis Chiappé about discovering the titanosaur nursery: www.amnh.org/exhibitions/expeditions/dinosaur/patagonia/environment.html

*Uncover T. Rex* by Dennis Schatz (Silver Dolphin Books, 2003)

*The Complete Dinosaur* by James O. Farlow and M. K. Brett-Surman (Indiana University Press, 1999)

**Dinosaur hunter**
Looks for dinosaur bones. Some hunters study the bones that they find themselves; others sell them or bring them back to be prepared in a laboratory and then studied in detail by paleontologists.

**Excavator**
Digs things out of the ground.

**Ichnologist**
Studies footprints and tracks. Such work is especially valuable for studying the lifestyles of dinosaurs.

**Professor**
A college or university teacher of the highest rank.

See the best collection of North American dinosaurs at: Royal Tyrrell Museum Drumheller
Alberta T0J 0Y0, Canada
Phone: (403) 823-8899
www.tyrrellmuseum.com

View *Tyrannosaurus rex* skeletons at:
Black Hills Museum of Natural History
117 Main Street
Hill City, SD 57745
Phone: (605) 574-4505
www.bhmnh.org

Find out more about the Dinosaur National Monument at:
The Dinosaur Quarry Visitor Center
Jensen, UT 84035
Phone: (435) 781-7700
www.nps.gov/dino/

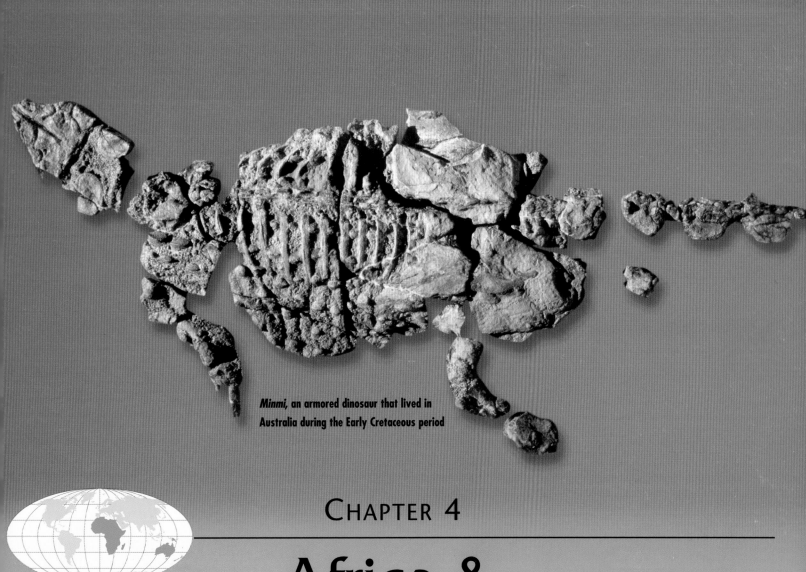

*Minmi,* an armored dinosaur that lived in Australia during the Early Cretaceous period

CHAPTER 4

# Africa & Australia

Africa and Australia were part of the southern landmass of Gondwanaland in dinosaur times. While Gondwanaland was part of the bigger supercontinent of Pangaea, the dinosaurs that lived there were similar to those in other parts of the world. However, as time went on and Gondwanaland separated from Laurasia, these southern dinosaurs developed different species from those in the north.

For a long time, dinosaurs had been found on every continent of the world except Antarctica. However, since the 1970s, dinosaur fossils have been found on the great Antarctic continent. Of course, at the time of the dinosaurs, Antarctica was not the frozen icecap that it is now. However, the dinosaur fossils found in southern Australia show that some dinosaurs were adapted to very cold conditions.

# Dinosaur teeth

Carnivorous dinosaurs evolved efficient meat slicers long before the invention of steak knives. A serrated edge is best for slicing through flesh. The largest predatory dinosaurs, such as North Africa's *Carchardontosaurus*, housed their teeth in massive jaws. *Carchardontosaurus* had a mouth that was large enough to hold a seven-year-old child, and some of its teeth were the length of a human hand. This four-ton predator's slashing bite would have been devastating.

### Teeth for plants

Plant-eating dinosaurs had different types of teeth. Prosauropods' teeth were coarsely serrated, like bread knives. Sauropods raked leaves from trees with comblike teeth. Ornithischians had beaks for gathering food and teeth that could either grind or chop. Ornithischians also had cheeks to hold the food while chewing.

▼ This *Carchardontosaurus* skull is shown beside a human skull for scale. *Carchardontosaurus* was a terrifying meat eater that chased its prey, pounding along on gigantic, muscular hind legs.

▼ Paul Sereno shows off the fossilized *Sarcosuchus* skeleton that he discovered in the Sahara. "Supercroc" was the length of a bus and probably weighed eight tons.

## Supercroc

Fifty years before Paul Sereno found a complete *Sarcosuchus* skeleton, French paleontologist Albert-Félix de Lapparent (1905–1975) found fossilized crocodile teeth in the Sahara. How did he know that they came from a giant crocodile and not a meat-eating dinosaur? Easy! Crocodile teeth are straight, while most dinosaur teeth are curved—but both types are just as good at killing and ripping up big prey. In Cretaceous times the Sahara was not a desert. It was a tropical plain, crisscrossed by tree-lined rivers and streams. It was also home to plenty of dinosaurs on which *Sarcosuchus* could feast.

▶ Like this modern crocodile, *Sarcosuchus* had upward-pointing eye sockets, so it probably relied on the same hunting technique. It would have waited just beneath the surface, ready to ambush dinosaurs and other prey that came to the riverbank to drink.

# Fast-moving plant eaters

During the Jurassic period, southern Africa was brutally hot. Most of the dinosaurs that lived there were small, dog-size plant eaters. *Lesothosaurus* and its close relative, *Fabrosaurus*, were bird-hipped dinosaurs that could run fast on their hind legs, using their long tails to stay balanced. *Heterodontosaurus* was another small, agile plant eater.

**Scrubland plants**
Early Jurassic southern Africa was a semidesert with a sparse, scrubby covering of cycads, conifers, and ferns. The supercontinent of Pangaea still existed, and inland climates could be harsh and hot. Certain dinosaurs may have estivated—slept during the hottest times of the year. Some scientists suggest that the teeth of *Heterodontosaurus* could not have grown correctly unless there were long estivation periods when they were not being used.

▲ In the open landscapes of the Early Jurassic, danger could be seen coming from a long distance away. Early plant eaters, such as *Lesothosaurus*, evolved long legs to run to safety.

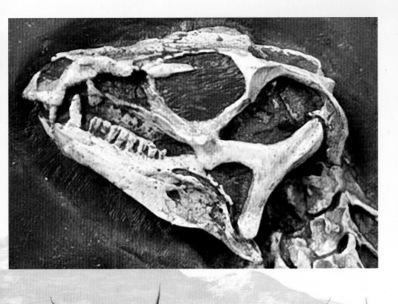

## Lumbering plant eaters

Not all of the Early Jurassic plant eaters were small and speedy. Prosauropods, relatives of the huge sauropods, appeared in Africa around this time. *Massospondylus* was a cow-size prosauropod, able to walk on all fours or up on its hind legs. It had teeth adapted for shredding plant matter, and it also swallowed stones that helped pulp tough vegetable fibers in its gizzard (prestomach).

◄ This skull belongs to *Heterodontosaurus*, or "different tooth lizard." The dinosaur had small teeth at the front of its mouth for snipping off leaves and stems and tall square ones at the back for grinding up plant fibers. It also had two pairs of longer teeth, or tusks, possibly for fighting rivals.

▲ As well as being equipped with three types of teeth, *Heterodontosaurus* may have also had cheek pouches. It could have used the pouches to push plant matter over its back teeth.

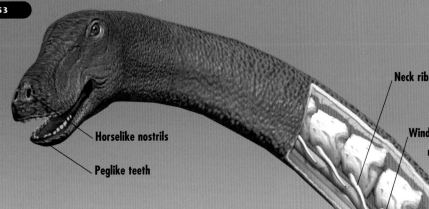

Horselike nostrils

Peglike teeth

Neck rib

Windpipe protected by
muscles and neck ribs

▼ *Rapetosaurus* did not chew its food. Instead, like all
sauropods, it swallowed stones in order to grind up the plant
food in its stomach. Modern plant-eating birds also do this.
We can find out about dinosaur food and digestion by looking
at fossil teeth and coprolite (fossil dung).

Muscles from
shoulder blade
power front leg

Gizzard

Huge lungs for
extracting oxygen
from air

Heart for pumping
oxygen-rich blood
around the body

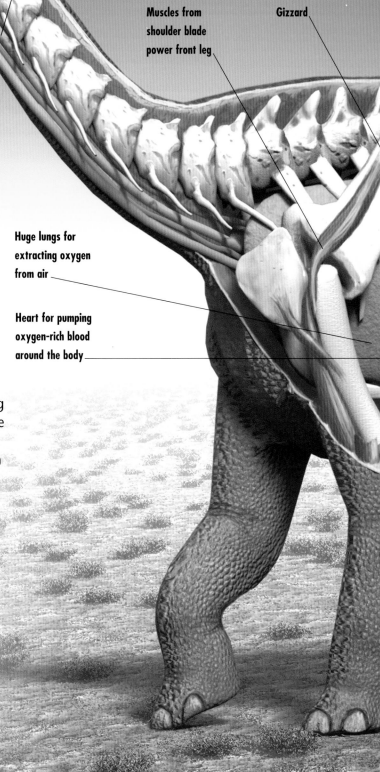

# Madagascan giant

Titanosaurs were sauropods that
flourished over most of the world for
200 million years. They had long necks
and tails, and they browsed on leafy
vegetation. Paleontologists have identified
more than 30 types of titanosaurs, but
almost all are known from only a few
bones. The most complete titanosaur
specimen was a skeleton of *Rapetosaurus*,
found on the island of Madagascar.

## Brain power

Relative to its body size, a titanosaur's brain was small. Finding
food did not demand much brain power because plants were
plentiful. *Rapetosaurus* needed some intelligence to evade
predators, but mostly it relied on its size. Growth patterns in
the bones show that, by the time that it was 12 years old, it
was too big for most meat eaters. *Tyrannosaurus* and other
hunters needed much bigger brains relative to their size so
that they could outwit their food—other dinosaurs!

## Bulky burden

Sauropods were the biggest-ever land animals. Experts
originally thought that they must have inhabited swamps
and lakes, where water could support their bulk. Now we
know that they did walk on land, because of fossil track
ways and bones found in dry habitats. Some
paleontologists argue that sauropods had air sacs, like
modern birds. Air sacs make birds' lungs more efficient
and also save weight, replacing some of the bone mass
with air. If sauropods had air sacs, their bodies would
have been much lighter than they had appeared.

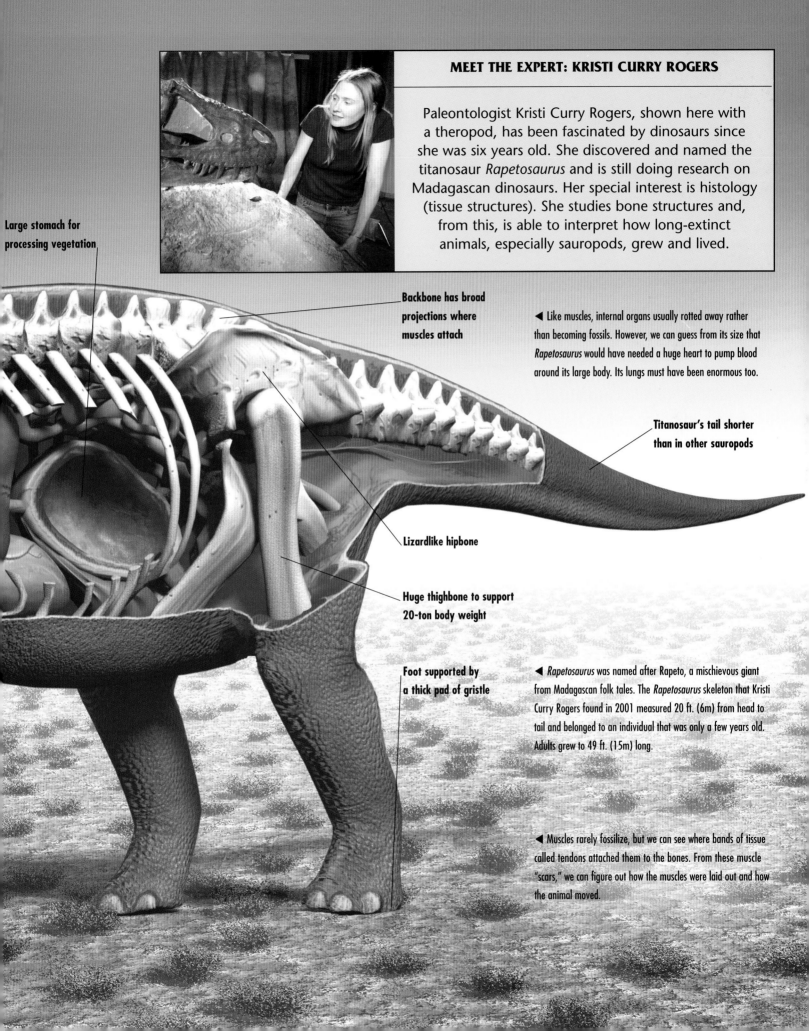

Large stomach for processing vegetation

Backbone has broad projections where muscles attach

◄ Like muscles, internal organs usually rotted away rather than becoming fossils. However, we can guess from its size that *Rapetosaurus* would have needed a huge heart to pump blood around its large body. Its lungs must have been enormous too.

Titanosaur's tail shorter than in other sauropods

Lizardlike hipbone

Huge thighbone to support 20-ton body weight

Foot supported by a thick pad of gristle

◄ *Rapetosaurus* was named after Rapeto, a mischievous giant from Madagascan folk tales. The *Rapetosaurus* skeleton that Kristi Curry Rogers found in 2001 measured 20 ft. (6m) from head to tail and belonged to an individual that was only a few years old. Adults grew to 49 ft. (15m) long.

◄ Muscles rarely fossilize, but we can see where bands of tissue called tendons attached them to the bones. From these muscle "scars," we can figure out how the muscles were laid out and how the animal moved.

# Dinosaur tracks

Australia has some of the best fossilized dinosaur tracks in the world, including very rare stegosaur prints. The track ways at Broome, Western Australia, and Lark Quarry, Queensland, have thousands of dinosaur prints. Ichnology—the study of fossil tracks—reveals a lot about dinosaur behavior.

**small ornithopod**

### Studying tracks

When footprints of many individuals of the same type of dinosaur are often found together, it shows that they lived in herds. Long track ways can indicate that dinosaurs migrated for hundreds or thousands of miles. The track way in Broome covers a 50-mi. (80-km) stretch of coastline. We cannot tell exactly what animals made the prints, but we can see what types of dinosaurs were involved. The biggest prints, which are 31 in. (80cm) long, were made by massive sauropods. There were also 21-in. (53-cm)-long prints from big theropods, prints from small, active ornithopods, and a set that may have come from a stegosaur.

**small theropod**

## Lark Quarry

In the 1960s, thousands of fossil footprints were found in Lark Quarry, Queensland, by a local farmer. The quarry was named after Malcolm Lark, a volunteer who helped excavate the site. The footprints tell about herds of small ornithopods (similar to *Hypsilophodon*) and small unidentified theropods drinking from a Cretaceous stream. Suddenly, they were spooked by the appearance of a big predator (a tyrannosaur), and they ran off in confusion, scattering in a frenzied stampede.

◄ The footprints in the sandstone of Lark Quarry look like a jumbled mess. However, after careful study, scientists have managed to piece together a dramatic story depicting herds of dinosaurs fleeing in panic from a hunter.

**tyrannosaur**

### FOOTPRINT SHAPES

Ornithopods walked on two legs. Their footprints have three toes, a lot like those of theropods, but with blunter claws.

Theropods stood on their hind legs and could run fast. Their prints showed three long toes like birds, their descendants.

Sauropods walked on all fours with their tails up, not sweeping the ground. The biggest prints are almost 5 ft. (1.5m) wide.

# Polar dinosaurs

In dinosaur times, the poles were warmer than they are today, although they were still cold. Polar dinosaurs had to cope with months of darkness, lit only by the moon and eerie southern lights. Dinosaur Cove, near Melbourne, Australia, is a time capsule of fossils that formed when Australia was farther south and within the Antarctic Circle. Since the 1970s, paleontologists have also discovered dinosaur fossils in Antarctica.

▲ A dinosaur warning sign stands by the road that leads to Dinosaur Cove. The dinosaurs that lived there 100 million years ago were very different from the *Stegosaurus* shown on the sign. They had evolved special ways of surviving the cold and the long, dark winters.

### MEET THE EXPERT:
### PATRICIA VICKERS-RICH

The excavations at Dinosaur Cove were led by geologist and paleontologist Patricia Vickers-Rich and her husband, Tom Rich, the curator of the Museum of Victoria. They named one of their major discoveries *Leaellynasaura* after their daughter Leaellyn and another *Timimus* after their son Tim.

## Dinosaur Cove

The Dinosaur Cove fossils were in very hard layers of rock, halfway up a cliff. The paleontologists blasted their way into the cliff face using explosives and heavy mining equipment. These Cretaceous rocks formed on the floor of a rift valley as Australia tore itself away from the continent of Antarctica, far to the south of where it now lies.

▲ In 2004, paleontologist William Hammer revisited the site on Antarctica's mainland where, 13 years earlier, he had discovered *Cryolophosaurus*, a crested meat-eating dinosaur from the Early Jurassic period. On this second expedition he found the remains of another, as yet unnamed, theropod.

◄ To gather every scrap of light, *Leaellynasaura* had huge eyes, and the parts of its brain devoted to vision were enlarged. It had a long tail and a small head and arms—a lot like a kangaroo! It shared the polar gloom with the strange, armored *Atlascopcosaurus*, ostrichlike *Timimus*, and a small, unnamed allosaur.

## Antarctic finds

During the Mesozoic Era, Antarctica was farther north than it is today, and it had a warm, moist climate. There is not much of Antarctica that is not covered by ice, so it is difficult to get to the rocks and fossils beneath the ground. However, since the 1980s, the bare, ice-free rocks of Vega Island, off the eastern side of the Antarctic peninsula, have yielded duck-billed dinosaurs and marine reptiles, while James Ross Island has produced a theropod and a nodosaurid ankylosaur. Perhaps the most spectacular find was that of the crested meat eater *Cryolophosaurus* on the mainland in 1991.

# SUMMARY OF CHAPTER 4: AFRICA & AUSTRALASIA

### The path of evolution

At the beginning of the age of the dinosaurs, the time of Pangaea, the dinosaurs on the modern continents of Africa, Australia, and Antarctica were not much different from those in other lands. The small, fast movers of southern Africa were similar to those of Europe and North America. In the Late Jurassic period, the dinosaurs of east Africa included huge sauropods such as *Brachiosaurus*, spiky stegosaurs such as *Kentrosaurus*, and fierce meat eaters such as *Allosaurus*—a similar mix to those of North America at the same time. Later, as the continents split up, dinosaurs began to evolve along their own separate lines. By the Cretaceous period, big plant eaters called titanosaurs lived on Madagascar (now an island off the southeastern coast of Africa). Like South America, where titanosaurs have also been found, Africa and Madagascar were part of the supercontinent of Gondwanaland at the time.

### An amazing mix

Not all of the big meat eaters were dinosaurs. *Sarcosuchus*, the biggest crocodile that the world has ever known, lived in Africa and probably fed on dinosaurs. Although we think of dinosaurs and other reptiles as being adapted to hot environments, we have found that the southern tip of Australia had a chilly Antarctic climate during Cretaceous times. But we have also discovered that this area had its own dinosaur population. Dinosaurs were more adaptable than originally thought.

The backbone of an Early Cretaceous plant eater, *Ouranosaurus*, sticks out of the desert sand in Niger, Africa. Since the 1990s, there have been many exciting dinosaur discoveries in the Sahara.

# Go further . . .

An account of Australian dinosaurs: home.alphalink.com.au/~dannj/

See Antarctic dinosaurs at: antarcticsun.usap.gov/oldissues2002-2003/Sun111002/dinosaurs.html

*Dinosaur Atlas* by DK Publishing (Dorling Kindersley, 2006)

*Dinosaur Worlds: Rise of the Dinosaurs* by Don Lessem (Boyds Mill Press, 1996)

**Histologist**
Studies tissues, especially bone tissues, to discover information about growth rates. Histology reveals how long dinosaurs lived and even in what type of conditions (bones may stop growing for a period of time if food is scarce or the climate is cold).

**Paleobiologist**
Studies the origins of life and the growth and structure of fossil animals as living organisms.

**Volunteer**
Works for no money—just for the interest of the job. Volunteers often work at dig sites.

Mounted skeletons from east Africa can be seen at: Humboldt Museum of Natural History
Berlin, Germany
Phone: +49 (0)30 2093 8591
www.naturkundemuseum-berlin.de

See early African dinosaurs at:
South African Museum
Cape Town, South Africa
Phone: +27 (0)21 481 3800
www.iziko.org.za/sam

The best place to see Australian dinosaurs is:
National Dinosaur Museum
Nicholls, Australia
Phone: +61 (0)2 6230 2655
www.nationaldinosaurmuseum.com.au

# TIMELINE

| | | | | |
|---|---|---|---|---|
| **MESOZOIC ERA** | **CRETACEOUS PERIOD** | **65 m.y.a.** | End of the age of reptiles. Dinosaurs, pterosaurs, swimming reptiles, and many other groups suddenly die out. Other types of animals are also badly hit: birds and marsupial mammals each lose 75 percent of their species, while placental mammals lose 14 percent. Despite these losses, birds and mammals eventually recover to repopulate the world. | **Tyrannosaurus rex** |
| | | **80 m.y.a.** | The continents are well scattered, with more individual landmasses than today. Different types of dinosaurs appear on different landmasses, evolving in isolation from each other. South America is an island continent. Eastern and western North America are separated by a shallow ocean, but western North America is still attached to Asia. | **Protoceratops** |
| | | **100 m.y.a.** | Flowering plants become widespread. The main type of landscape is forests of broadleaved trees with an undergrowth of floral herbs. Dinosaurs evolve into ground-feeding and low-browsing types such as duckbills, ceratopsians, and armored dinosaurs. Coniferous trees—and the high-browsing dinosaurs that feed on them—become restricted to upland areas. | **Tenontosaurus** |
| | | **120 m.y.a.** | The climate is warm and moist. Gondwanaland breaks up as South America separates from Africa, and India separates from Australia and Antarctica. The sea level is generally low, but it begins to rise as the period progresses. Different types of birds evolve, especially in China, which is also home to feathered dinosaurs such as *Microraptor*. | **Microraptor** |
| | **JURASSIC PERIOD** | **145 m.y.a.** | The end of the Jurassic period and the beginning of the Cretaceous. This is the heyday of the long-necked, plant-eating sauropods such as *Brachiosaurus* and of the tall coniferous trees on which they feed. An extinction in the oceans marks the end of the Jurassic, with around 30 percent of species dying out. Birds evolve from theropod dinosaurs. | **Brachiosaurus** |
| | | **160 m.y.a.** | The South Atlantic Ocean begins to open up, creating rift valleys in Gondwanaland. North America remains connected to Europe by a land bridge. The sea level is quite high, with many shallow coastal seas and a wide variety of marine animals. The Rocky Mountains begin to rise. Climates are generally moist. Theropods, such as *Megalosaurus*, are the main predators. | **Megalosaurus** |
| | | **175 m.y.a.** | Sudden flourishing of the long-necked sauropods and the large meat eaters that prey upon them. Insects, such as dragonflies and cockroaches, are plentiful. The Tethys Ocean separates Pangaea into Laurasia and Gondwanaland. This ocean is home to various marine reptiles such as ichthyosaurs, which had first appeared 250 million years ago. | **Ichthyosaurus** |
| | | **180 m.y.a.** | New ammonite species appear, following the end-Triassic extinction. Dinosaurs flourish and take the places of other reptile groups. Among the dinosaurs, plated stegosaurs appear as well as the two-legged heterodontosaurs. Inland climates remain dry, especially in North America and southern Africa. | **Scelidosaurus** |
| | **TRIASSIC PERIOD** | **208 m.y.a.** | End of the Triassic period and beginning of the Jurassic. Mass extinction affects 65 percent of marine species and a large number of land species. The first true mammals appear and survive the extinction. Pangaea is still in one piece, but the Tethys Ocean partly separates it into a northern part, Laurasia, and a southern part, Gondwanaland. | **Morganucodon** |
| | | **210 m.y.a.** | Flying archosaurs called pterosaurs appear. Conifers become the main plant form as seed ferns die out. Reptiles that feed on the seed ferns also decline, allowing the dinosaurs to flourish. Rift valleys begin to appear across Pangaea. Crocodile-like reptiles include groups that will become extinct at the end of the Triassic such as rauisuchians like the 16-ft. (5-m)-long *Prestosuchus*. | **Prestosuchus** |
| | | **230 m.y.a.** | Seed ferns take over from the club mosses as the main plants. The center of Pangaea is so far from the ocean that it is arid and lifeless. Life flourishes around the edges of the continent, where the climate is seasonal. Archosaurs begin to split into the crocodile group and the dinosaur group, which includes *Eoraptor* (one of the earliest-known dinosaurs). | **Eoraptor** |
| | | **250 m.y.a.** | Beginning of the Triassic period. All of the landmasses are joined in the supercontinent of Pangaea. Animal life is recovering after a mass extinction at the end of the Permian period, which wiped out up to 95 percent of species. Archosaurs are the main surviving group of reptiles. As in the preceding periods, the most widespread plants are the club mosses. | **Club moss** |

# Glossary

**ammonite**
An extinct shellfish with a coiled shell that was common in the Mesozoic Era.

**ankylosaur**
An armored ornithischian dinosaur that had bony plates on its back.

**badlands**
Areas of wasteland and worn-away rock, which are literally "bad lands" to cross.

**belemnite**
An extinct shellfish with a bullet-shaped shell that was common in the Mesozoic Era.

**camouflage**
A color or pattern that makes something difficult to see against its background.

**carnivore**
A flesh-eating animal.

**ceratopsian**
An ornithischian dinosaur that had a head shield and sometimes horns.

**climate**
The average weather conditions of an area over a long period of time.

**cold-blooded**
Describes an animal that cannot control its body temperature. Fish, amphibians, and modern reptiles are cold-blooded.

**comet**
A space body made of ice and rock.

**conifer**
An evergreen tree that reproduces by cones—for example, pine and cypress.

**coprolite**
Fossilized dung.

**Cretaceous**
The time from 145 to 65 million years ago and the third of the three periods that make up the Mesozoic Era.

**cycad**
A primitive plant related to conifers but resembling a palm tree.

**dromaeosaur**
A small theropod dinosaur with an outsize claw on each hind foot.

**duckbill**
An ornithopod dinosaur that had a ducklike beak and, usually, a head crest.

**environment**
The total conditions of a place—its landscape, climate, plants, and animal life.

**estivate**
To spend the hot summer months sleeping.

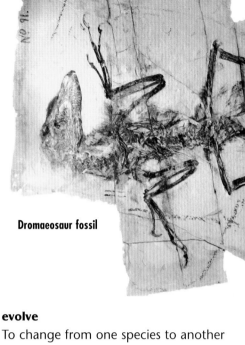

Dromaeosaur fossil

**evolve**
To change from one species to another over millions of years by passing on useful characteristics from one generation to the next.

**extinct**
Describes an animal or plant that has died out globally, never to reappear.

**fossil**
The remains of an animal or plant that died long ago, preserved in rock.

**gizzard**
In some dinosaurs and birds, a muscular pouch that holds swallowed stones in order to to grind food before it enters the stomach.

**Gondwanaland**
The southern landmass created by the breakup of Pangaea.

**ichthyosaur**
A dolphinlike, predatory marine reptile that lived in the Mesozoic Era.

**Jurassic**
The time from 206 to 145 million years ago and the second of the three periods that make up the Mesozoic Era.

*Tyrannosaurus* skeleton

**ornithopod**
A two-legged ornithischian dinosaur.

**paleontologist**
A scientist who studies fossils.

**Pangaea**
The supercontinent that existed from around 270 to 175 million years ago, made up of all the world's landmasses.

**placodont**
A turtlelike reptile from the Triassic period.

**plesiosaur**
A long-necked, predatory marine reptile that lived in the Jurassic and Cretaceous periods.

**pliosaur**
A short-necked marine reptile, related to plesiosaurs, that lived in the Mesozoic Era.

**prosauropod**
A large, long-necked, plant-eating saurischian dinosaur that walked on two legs or on all fours.

**pterosaur**
A flying reptile with wings made from skin stretched over a long fourth finger.

**saurischian**
Describes the group of dinosaurs that had hipbones arranged like those of a lizard. The saurischians were made up of theropods (which gave rise to birds) and sauropods.

**sauropod**
A huge, long-necked, plant-eating saurischian dinosaur that walked on all fours, related to the prosauropods.

**stegosaur**
An ornithischian dinosaur that had plates on its back.

**supercontinent**
A landmass containing more than one continental plate.

**KT boundary**
The rock layer that marks the time when dinosaurs became extinct, the end of the Cretaceous, and beginning of the Tertiary.

**Laurasia**
The northern landmass created by the breakup of Pangaea.

**Mesozoic Era**
The period of geological time stretching from 251 to 65 million years ago.

**metabolism**
The physical and chemical systems that keep an animal or plant alive.

**mosasaur**
A giant, predatory marine lizard that lived in the Cretaceous period.

**nothosaur**
A fish-eating marine reptile that lived in Triassic oceans.

**ornithischian**
Describes the group of dinosaurs that had hipbones arranged like those of a bird. The ornithischians were made up of the ornithopods, pachycephalosaurs, ceratopsians, stegosaurs, and ankylosaurs. They were all plant eaters.

**Tertiary**
The period of geological time after the Mesozoic Era, from 65 to two million years ago.

**theropod**
A two-legged, carnivorous saurischian dinosaur with sharp teeth and claws.

**Triassic**
The time from 251 to 206 million years ago and the first of the three periods that make up the Mesozoic Era, when early dinosaurs appeared.

**tyrannosaur**
A large, flesh-eating theropod dinosaur.

*Eoraptor* skull

**vertebrate**
An animal with a backbone.

**volcano**
A hole (vent) through which gas, ash, and molten rock erupt onto Earth's surface and may build up to form a mountain.

**warm-blooded**
Describes an animal that can keep its body temperature the same, regardless of the surrounding temperature. Birds and mammals are warm-blooded.

# Index

Alaska 29
allosaurs 35, 57
*Allosaurus* 9, 46, 58
*Amargasaurus* 34
Andrews, Roy Chapman 20, 21
ankylosaurs 9, 32, 57
Anning, Mary 16, 17
Antarctica 47, 56, 57
*Apatosaurus* 17, 46
*Archaeopteryx* 25
Argentina 29, 34, 42, 46
*Argentinosaurus* 34, 35, 46
armor 9, 14, 32–33, 38, 46, 59
*Atlascopcosaurus* 57
*Aucasaurus* 42
Australia 10, 32, 47, 54, 55, 56, 57
*Avisaurus* 39

badlands 36, 46
*Bambiraptor* 44
beaks 14, 21, 25, 31, 39, 40, 48
Belgium 15, 17
bird-hipped dinosaurs *see*
    ornithischians
bird mimics *see* ornithomimids
birds 13, 15, 23, 28, 38, 39, 59
body heat 20, 22, 24, 44–45
*Brachiosaurus* 8, 58, 59
*Brachychampsa* 38
brains 30, 52, 57
Brazil 29
Buckland, William 16, 28
*Buitreraptor* 35

Canada 29
*Carchardontosaurus* 48
*Centrosaurus* 32
cerapods 9
ceratopsians 9, 10, 11, 20, 32, 36,
    38, 39, 59
characteristics 8
China 15, 22, 28
claws 20, 25, 30, 46
climates 10, 11, 38, 50, 57, 59
Collini, Cosimo 17

comets 12
communication 41
*Compsognathus* 8, 23
continents 10–11, 14, 47, 58, 59
Cope, Edward 16, 29
crests 40, 41
crocodiles 38, 58, 59
*Cryolophosaurus* 57
Cuvier, Georges 16

Dakota 13, 45
*Deinonychus* 30, 31
*Deinosuchus* 41
digestion 9, 52
digs 18–19
Dinosaur Cove 56, 57
*Diplodocus* 44
*Draco* lizards 24
dromaeosaurs 23, 30, 31, 36
*Dromaeosaurus* 30
*Dsungaripterus* 25
duck-billed dinosaurs (hadrosaurs)
    10, 36, 38, 39, 46, 57, 59

*Edmontosaurus* 39, 40
eggs 18, 21, 27, 28, 41, 42, 43
*Elasmosaurus* 27
*Eoraptor* 59
estivation 50
*Euoplocephalus* 32
Everglades 38
excavation 18-19
extinction 12–13, 14, 59
eyelids 32
eyesight 37, 57

*Fabrosaurus* 50
families 8–9
feathers 20, 22–23, 59
fighting 20–21, 22
flight 22, 23, 24–25
flippers 26
Florida 38
footprints 36, 54, 55
fossil hunters 16, 21

fossils 14, 18–19, 20, 21, 26, 28, 29,
    34, 46, 47, 57
France 16

*Giganotosaurus* 35, 46
gigantothermic 44
gliders 22, 23, 24
Gobi desert 15, 18, 20, 21, 28
Gondwanaland 10, 47, 58, 59
Great Britain 16

hadrosaurs 40–41
    *see also* duck-billed dinosaurs
hearts 37, 44, 45, 53
Hell Creek 36–39, 46
*Helopanoplia* 39
herds 40, 41, 43, 46, 54, 55
*Heterodontosaurus* 50, 51
Horner, Jack 41
horns 9, 20, 28, 32, 33, 38, 46
hunting 23, 24, 27, 30, 31, 44,
    46, 49
*Hylaeosaurus* 28

ichthyosaurs 26, 27, 28, 59
*Iguanodon* 15, 16, 17, 28
insects 38, 39, 59
iridium 12, 13
*Istiodactylus* 25

jaws 16, 37, 40

*Kentrosaurus* 58
KT boundary 13

de Lapparent, Albert-Félix 49
Lark Quarry 54, 55
Laurasia 10, 47, 59
*Leaellynasaura* 57
*Lesothosaurus* 50
limbs 8, 14
lizard-hipped dinosaurs *see*
    saurischians
lungs 52, 53

Madagascar 52, 58
*Maiasaura* 41
Mantell, Gideon 16, 17, 28
marginocephalians 9
Marsh, Othniel 16, 17, 29
*Massospondylus* 51
meat eaters 9, 14, 16, 28, 35, 36, 37,
  38, 45, 46, 48, 57, 58, 59
*Megalosaurus* 16, 28, 59
metabolism 44
meteorites 12, 13, 14
Mexico 12
*Microraptor* 22, 59
migration 54
Mongolia 15, 20
Montana 36, 41, 46
mosasaurs 17, 26, 27, 28
muscles 53

nests 18, 41, 42, 43, 46
Netherlands, the 17
nodosaurs 32, 57
nothosaurs 26

ornithischians 9, 14, 48
ornithomimids 30, 31
ornithopods 9, 14, 46, 54, 55
*Ouranosaurus* 58
*Oviraptor* 18, 21
Owen, Sir Richard 15, 16, 28

pachycephalosaurs 9
paddles 27
Pangaea 10, 47, 50, 58, 59
*Parasaurolophus* 41
Patagonia 34, 42, 46
placodonts 26
plant eaters 9, 14, 20, 38, 45, 46, 48,
  50, 51, 58, 59
plants 11, 36, 38, 39, 50, 59
plesiosaurs 26, 27, 28
pliosaurs 26, 27
Portugal 16
predators 20, 30, 42, 45, 48
*Prestosuchus* 59
prosauropods 48, 51
prospecting 18
*Protarchaeopteryx* 23
*Protoceratops* 20, 21, 59

*Psittacosaurus* 15
*Pteranodon* 25
*Pterodaustro* 25
pterodactyls 24
pterosaurs 13, 17, 24-25, 29, 59

*Rapetosaurus* 52, 53
reptiles 8
rivers 38, 43, 46, 49
runners 9, 20, 30, 31, 37, 50, 55

Sahara 49, 58
*Saltasaurus* 42, 43
*Sarcosuchus* 49, 58
saurischians 9, 14
sauropods 9, 10, 14, 17, 34, 35, 46,
  48, 51, 52, 54, 55, 58, 59
scales 20, 22
scavengers 35
*Scelidosaurus* 59
sedimentary rock 24, 26
Sereno, Paul 49
shellfish 13
*Sinosauropteryx* 22, 23
skin 22, 40
spines 34
stegosaurs 9, 54, 58, 59
*Stegosaurus* 9
*Struthiomimus* 31
*Styracosaurus* 32
swamps 38, 52
swimming 26, 27

tail clubs 32
tails 24, 35, 53, 57
*Tarbosaurus* 20
teeth 16, 20, 25, 30, 35, 37, 40, 46,
  48, 49, 51
*Tenontosaurus* 30, 59
theropods 9, 13, 14, 35, 54, 55,
  57, 59
*Thescelosaurus* 37, 46
thyreophorans 9
*Timimus* 56
titanosaurs 52
tracks 54
track ways 36, 52, 54–55
trees 38, 39, 59
*Triceratops* 10, 11, 32, 33, 36, 38

*Troodon* 30, 36
turtles 26, 27
tyrannosaurs 34, 55
*Tyrannosaurus rex* 9, 32, 34, 35, 36,
  37, 38, 44, 46, 52, 59

United States 16, 36, 37, 38, 45

*Velociraptor* 20, 21
vertebrae 34
volcanoes 13, 22

wings 22, 23, 24, 25

*Xianglong* 24

young 41, 42, 43

# Acknowledgments

The publisher would like to thank the following for permission to reproduce their material. Every care has been taken to trace copyright holders. However, if there have been unintentional omissions or failure to trace copyright holders, we apologize and will, if informed, endeavor to make corrections in any future edition.

Key: *b* = bottom, *c* = center, *l* = left, *r* = right, *t* = top

1 Natural History Museum, London; 2–3 Corbis/Louie Psihoyos; 7 Dean Steadman/Kingfisher; 13*tl* Corbis/Walter Geiersperger; 13*tr* Dean Steadman/Kingfisher; 13*cr* Photolibrary/Jeremy Woodhouse; 14 Getty/National Geographic Society; 15 Loïc Bazalgette, Laboratoire Dynamique de la Lithosphère, Université Montpellier II; 16 Natural History Museum, London; 16–17 Corbis/Ladislav Janicek/zefa; 18*bl* Mike Hettwer; 18–19 Getty/Louie Psihoyos; 20*tl* Getty/AFP; 20*b* Natural History Museum, London; 21*t* American Museum of Natural History, Washington, D.C.; 22*t* Corbis/Xinhua; 22*b* Getty/Xu Xing; 24*bl* Photolibrary/Satoshi Kuribayashi; 25 Science Photo Library/Jim Amos; 27 Natural History Museum, London; 28 Natural History Museum, London; 29 Getty/Richard Nowitz; 30 DK Images; 31 Dean Steadman/Kingfisher; 33*tr* Science Photo Library/Smithsonian Institution; 34 Don Lessum, Dino Don Inc.; 34*tr* Empics/AP/Mariano Izquierdo; 35 Science Photo Library/Carlos Goldin; 36 Dean Steadman/Kingfisher; 36–37 Dean Steadman/Kingfisher; 37 Empics/AP/Karen Tam; 37*b* Corbis/Louie Psihoyos; 40–41 Impossible Pictures; 40*bl* Natural History Museum, London; 41*t* Natural History Museum, London; 42*bl* Corbis/Louie Psihoyos; 44 Science Photo Library/Christian Darkin; 45 Jim Page/North Carolina Museum of Natural Sciences; 46 Getty/Louie Psihoyos; 47 Queensland Museum, Australia; 48*bl* Getty/Louie Psihoyos; 48–49 Empics/AP/Rick Bowmer; 49*t* Corbis/Sygma; 49*b* Science Photo Library/Tom McHugh; 51*t* University of California Museum of Paleontology; 53 Empics/AP/Gail Burton; 54–55 Wildlight/Philip Quirk; 55*t* Corbis/John Noble; 56*bl* AAP Image/Julian Smith; 56 Corbis/Frans Lanting; 56*tr* Science Photo Library/Peter Menzel; 57*t* Empics/AP/Augustane College; 58*b* Getty/Stephen Wilkes; 58–59*t* Getty/AFP; 59*br* Corbis/Louie Psihoyos; 62–63 Loïc Bazalgette, Laboratoire Dynamique de la Lithosphère, Université Montpellier II; 64 Getty/Louie Psihoyos.

The publisher would like to thank the following illustrators: Rebecca Painter 9*br*, 36*cl*, 55*b*; Sebastien Quigley (Linden Artists) 18–19; Sam Weston (Linden Artists) 8–9, 12–13, 16–17, 24–25, 26–27, 38–39, 42–43, 50–51; Sam Weston and Steve Weston (Linden Artists) 20–21, 34–35; Steve Weston (Linden Artists) cover, 4–5, 11, 22–23, 30–31, 32–33, 44–45*c*, 52–53, 54–55, 56–57; Peter Winfield 10, 15, 17*r*, 19*r*, 26*b*, 29, 45*r*, 47, 59.

The publisher would also like to thank Kristi Curry Rogers for her assistance with pages 52–53 and David Varrichio for his assistance with page 18.